BLUEPRINTS
Sounds For Reading

Frances James **Ann Kerr**

Stanley Thornes (Publishers) Ltd

Stanley Thornes for TEACHERS:
BLUEPRINTS • PRIMARY COLOURS • LEARNING TARGETS

Stanley Thornes for Teachers publishes practical teacher's ideas books and photocopiable resources for use in primary schools. Our three key series, **Blueprints**, **Primary Colours** and **Learning Targets** together provide busy teachers with unbeatable curriculum coverage, inspiration and value for money. We mail teachers and schools about our books regularly. To join the mailing list simply photocopy and complete the form below and return using the **FREEPOST** address to receive regular updates on our new and existing titles. You may also like to add the name of of friend who would be interested in being on the mailing list. Books can be bought by credit card over the telephone and information obtained on (01242) 267280.

Please add my name to the **Stanley Thornes for TEACHERS** mailing list.

Mr/Mrs/Miss/Ms _____

Address _____

_____ postcode _____

School address _____

_____ postcode _____

Please also send information about **Stanley Thornes for TEACHERS** to:

Mr/Mrs/Miss/Ms _____

Address _____

_____ postcode _____

To: Marketing Services Dept., Stanley Thornes Ltd, FREEPOST (GR 782), Cheltenham, GL50 1BR

Text © Frances James, Ann Kerr 1998.

The right of Frances James and Ann Kerr to be identified as authors of this work has been asserted by them in accordance with the Copyright, Designs and Patents Act 1988.

The copyright holders authorise ONLY users of Blueprints: Sounds for Reading to make photocopies or stencil duplicates of the Copymasters for their own or their classes' immediate use within the teaching context. No rights are granted without permission in writing from the Copyright Licensing Agency of Tottenham Court Road, London W1P 9HE.

First published in 1998 by
Stanley Thornes Publishers Ltd
Ellenborough House
Wellington Street
Cheltenham GL50 1YW

98 99 00 01 02 / 10 9 8 7 6 5 4 3 2 1

A catalogue record for this book is available from the British Library.

ISBN 0-7487-3729-4

Typeset by Aetos Ltd, Bath

Printed and Bound in Great Britain by Redwood Books, Trowbridge, Wiltshire.

Contents

Introduction	5
Using this book with the National Curriculum	8
Listening skills Copymasters 1–10	11
Knowledge of letters and words Copymasters 11–25	25
Syllables Copymasters 26–32	45
Rhymes and rhyming words Copymasters 33–62	55
Alliteration Copymasters 63–70	91
Onset and rime Copymasters 71–81	101
Analogy Copymasters 82–84	115
Individual phonemes Copymasters 85–90	119
Assessment	126

INTRODUCTION

What this book is about

Blueprints: Sounds for Reading is a practical classroom resource designed to help infant and early years teachers teach essential basic phonic skills that all children need in order to go on to become fluent readers. The book contains practical activities plus 90 worksheets which focus on these key early phonological skills. These include the following:
- vital basic listening skills
- an understanding of the difference between words and letters
- the ability to hear separate syllables in words
- learning to hear and generate rhymes and alliterations
- learning about onsets and rimes
- learning to use analogy to help with reading
- learning to hear individual phonemes in words

The book does not go so far as teaching children to blend letters together to make words. This would be the next, further stage of development.

The ideas and developmental sequence of the book is based upon the now widely accepted thinking about how children best learn about sounds. You will find that it uses the new terminology of phonic teaching which may be unfamiliar to some teachers; for example it uses concepts such as grapheme, phoneme, onset and rime. The content of the book is fully in line with the demands of The National Literacy Strategy and you will find an National Literacy Strategy planner on pages 8/9. It is also in line with the demands for early phonic learning of Scotland 5-14 English Language Guidelines and the curriculum for Northern Ireland.

Phonological skills and learning to read

It is now generally accepted that fluent readers use four strategies: visual (recognising words by sight), semantic (using their knowledge of context), syntactic (using their knowledge of grammar) and phonic (the relationship between spoken sounds and letters).

The strategy that has attracted the most attention has been the teaching of phonics but the fervent debate about whether children should be explicitly taught about the relationship of letters and their associated sounds seems to have been largely resolved. There has been disquiet amongst teachers about teaching simple initial letter-sound correspondences to reception children. This approach often led to greater confusion and teachers were faced with the challenge of explaining the frequent exceptions or inconsistencies in English to young children. It sometimes seemed easier to ignore the issue even though it was indisputable that children needed to know about the relationships of spoken sounds and letters to enable them to decode unfamiliar words, to learn common letter strings and to develop spelling strategies.

Recent research has provided considerable insight into ways in which phonics can be taught to children within a developmental framework which will provide them with these vital skills. The research has broadened the approach from a narrow focus on phonemic relationships to a broader perspective which addresses the phonology of English, the overall sound system of the language.

Words can be regarded as the largest phonological units of language and they can then be broken into ever smaller phonological units: syllables, rimes, onsets and phonemes as follows:

Word	Syllables	Rime	Onset	Phonemes
pig	pig	ig	p	p-i-g
fair	fair	air	f	f-ai-r
window	win	in	w	w-i-n
	dow	ow	d	d-ow

Syllables are denoted by the internal rhythm or beats in words; they are characterised by peaks of acoustic energy. Rimes and onsets are phonological divisions within monosyllabic words or syllables. The rime is the part of the syllable that allows it to rhyme with other syllables and the onset is the initial phoneme or blend.

Phonemes are the smallest units of sound. There are effectively 44 phonemes in English. The illustrations in the previous table highlight the need for accuracy when describing phonemes. In the word 'fair' for example, 'f' is identified as being the phoneme but it is in fact a grapheme, the written form of a phoneme. The other possible graphemes for this phoneme are 'ff (as in 'cuff'), 'ph' (as in 'photograph') and 'gh' (as in 'cough'). These have to be presented to children as spelling choices when they can hear the individual phonemes within words.

This structure provides a logical approach for developing the children's phonological knowledge. The children first have to learn to identify words from within a stream of speech. Once they appreciate the integrity of words they can begin to learn about the components leading, ultimately, to a detailed knowledge of phonemes.

The activities in this book

The activities in this book are presented in sections in a broadly developmental order. You will find a summary of the contents below. We begin with activities that are designed to enhance children's listening skills. Phonology is all to do with sound and it is self-evident that for children to be accomplished in this area they will need to have accurate listening skills to enable them to identify and discriminate sounds. The work on syllables is introduced by building upon the children's appreciation of rhythm and uses music to reinforce this concept.

Considerable attention is devoted to nursery rhymes. Bryant and Bradley's research (1985) demonstrated that children's knowledge of nursery rhymes is a strong indicator of their later reading skills. Nursery rhymes are an important part of the English literary tradition. Most nursery rhymes have a strong rhythm and they are a potent way of introducing the children to rhyming words. The appreciation of rhyme is essential if children are to learn about rimes. Alliteration is used to introduce onsets. With a firm understanding of rimes and onsets children are able to develop their sense of analogy to read and spell words that share common regular letter strings.

We have also included activities which address children's knowledge of letter names and alphabetical order. This may seem out of place in a book about phonology but there is considerable research evidence that suggests that children's ability to name letters is another indicator of their later reading ability. The advantage of letter names is that they are constant; phonemes associated with letters can change. If children can name letters this provides them with a tool by which they can remember and work with letters. We have included both lower case and capital letters because that reflects the children's experience; by teaching both lower case and capital letters specifically the chances that the children will be confused are lessened.

Phonology is all about sound and so we have stressed throughout the teacher's notes the importance of oral and aural activities. The activity sheets should not be seen as worksheets to be completed in silence. The children should be experimenting with and experiencing the sounds of and within words. They should be encouraged to play with language, noticing the rhythm, generating and recognising rhyme and alliteration.

The activities should be linked with real texts whenever possible. This approach to teaching phonology is built on the principle that it should be meaningful to the children. They should be able to relate what they are learning about sounds to their growing appreciation of text.

Learning outcomes are identified for each of the activities. These should be incorporated into any lesson or weekly plans, including those associated with the National Literacy Strategy. For some of the tasks extension activities are also described; these are designed to challenge the more able pupils. There are also ideas of how to support children who find the concepts more difficult. It is important to differentiate the activities. Some children will arrive in school or a nursery class with a good knowledge of nursery rhymes and letters, others will find accurate listening difficult.

Many of the activities can be completed with minimal adult support. Some of the activities have been designed for consolidation and reinforcement of specific concepts or skills.

Assessment
You may wish to use some of the activity sheets as assessment activities. We have included an assessment sheet at the end of the book to enable you to record the children's achievements. The assessment sheet is criterion-referenced and is expressed in a series of statements about what the children "can do". Use the assessment sheet as a tool for planning your next teaching steps with individual or groups of children. The first three small boxes can be used to tick when a pupil has undertaken a particular task and the final box used when the pupil can demonstrate mastery of the skill. Assessing each area can be undertaken by observation during normal classroom work, using the activity sheets or by devising simple tests for a particular skill. It will also help you track individual pupil's progress and identify any child who is experiencing particular problems. A checklist for recording the children's knowledge of the vocabulary associated with literacy is given below.

Reading Vocabulary Checklist
Word, letter, same, different, name, capital letter, lower case letter, first, last, middle, rhyme, syllable, consonant, vowel, phoneme, grapheme.

References
The following books underlie the content of this book.

Adams, M. J. *Beginning to Read: Learning and Thinking about Print* MIT Press (1990)

Bryant, P. E. and Bradley, L. *Children's Reading Difficulties*. Blackwells (1985)

DfEE *The National Literacy Strategy - Framework for Teaching* DfEE (1998)

Goswami, U. 'Reading by Analogy' in *Reading Development and Dyslexia* eds. Hulme, C. and Snowling, M. Whurr (1994)

Summary of contents
Listening Skills: Activity Sheets 1-10
This section is designed to heightened children's awareness of sounds in the environment and the aural features of words: the length of words and the different sounds within them. An emphasis is placed upon the rhythm of words through building on the children's knowledge of refrains in well-known stories.

Knowledge of words and letters: Activity sheets 11-25
These sheets explore the difference between words and letters. They use environmental print to introduce the difference between capital and lower case letters. There are a number of activities that aim to consolidate the children's knowledge of capital and lower case letters. Alphabetical order is introduced in this section,

Syllables: Activity sheets 26-32
Syllables are introduced by exploiting the internal rhythm in words. The activity sheets reinforce the

children's ability to count the number of syllables in words and to relate this knowledge to print.

Nursery rhymes and rhyming words: Activity sheets 33-62
Well-known nursery rhymes are used to introduce the children to the concept of rhyme and to enable them to identify and generate words that rhyme. Many of the activities use games to reinforce specific skills.

Alliteration: Activity sheets 63-70
The activity sheets are designed to increase the children's sensitivity to alliteration - words that share the same initial phonemes.

Onset and rime: Activity sheets 71-81

With a good aural knowledge of rhyme and alliteration children will be able to develop their appreciation of onsets and rimes and their relationship to print. The activity sheets in this section introduce the children to common rimes and onsets.

Analogy: Activity sheets 82-84
This section requires the children to use their sense of analogy to read and spell words which share common regular spelling patterns.

Individual phonemes: Activity sheets 85-90
The identification of individual phonemes in words demands sophisticated and sensitive listening skills. The sheets require the children to identify the number of phonemes in different words.

USING THIS BOOK WITH THE NATIONAL LITERACY STRATEGY

The approach to teaching phonology found in this book is embedded in the National Literacy Strategy (NLS). The NLS provides a detailed framework of teaching for the development of literacy from reception to year 6. The framework covers the statutory requirements for reading and writing in the National Curriculum for English and contributes substantially to the development of speaking and listening.

In the introduction to the NLS it states that literate primary pupils should:
- read and write with confidence, fluency and understanding;
- be able to orchestrate a full range of reading cues (phonic, graphic, syntactic, contextual) to monitor their reading and correct their own mistakes;
- understand the sound and spelling system and use this to read and spell accurately;
- have fluent and legible handwriting;
- have an interest in words and their meanings and a growing vocabulary;
- know, understand and be able to write in a range of genres in fiction and poetry, and understand and be familiar with some of the ways in which narratives are structured through basic literary ideas of setting, character and plot;
- understand, use and be able to write a range of non-fiction texts;
- plan, draft, revise and edit their own writing;
- have a suitable technical vocabulary through which to understand and discuss their reading and writing;
- be interested in books, read with enjoyment and evaluate and justify their preferences;
- through reading and writing, develop their powers of imagination, inventiveness and critical awareness.

The introduction also draws attention to the rather cautious approach to the teaching of phonics by many teachers. Although this is probably less true currently than in previous years, research clearly indicates that it is very important to teach children about the overall sound system in the English language. In the NLS there is a clear emphasis on the systematic teaching of phonics and other word level skills. It says pupils should be taught to:
- discriminate between the separate sounds in words;
- learn the letters and letter combinations most commonly used to spell those sounds;
- read words by sounding out and blending their separate parts;
- write words by combining the spelling patterns of their sounds.

The NLS also stresses the importance of the use of a range of meaningful text that is lively and interesting to pupils to support their acquisition of word attack skills. The range should include fiction, poetry, information and reference books. Big books, sets of reading books, graded individual reading books and a wide selection of non-fiction and reference books need to be available for the pupils.

The National Literacy Strategy must be taught each day in sessions of one hour. This hour comprises four components:
15 minutes whole class shared reading and writing;
15 minutes whole class word level work;
20 minutes guided group and independent work;
10 minutes whole class plenary session.

The Activity sheets and Extension activities in this book can be used for NLS hour teaching particularly with reception and year 1 pupils. They can be used as whole class, group or independent activities particularly for word level work. Some of the Activity sheets are preparation for later work, particularly the work on developing good listening skills. The NLS does not include this element in detail but it is essential that pupils have an opportunity to learn and practise these skills.

At reception and year 1 word level work in the NLS is summarised as follows:
- Phonological awareness, phonics and spelling
- Word recognition, graphic knowledge and spelling
- Vocabulary extension
- Handwriting

Cross-referencing to the National Literacy Strategy
The following is a cross reference between the NLS and the Activity sheets contained in this book:

Reception Year - phonological awareness, phonics and spelling
1 to understand and be able to rhyme through:
- recognising, exploring and working with rhyming patterns, e.g. learning nursery rhymes: Activity sheets 33-62
- extending these patterns by analogy, generating new and invented words in speech and spelling: Activity sheets 42-62, 82-84

2 knowledge of grapheme - phoneme correspondence through:
- hearing and identifying initial sounds in words; 9-10, 44-69

- reading letter(s) that represent(s) the sounds; 71-81, 88-90
- writing each letter in response to each sound; 71-75, 82-84
- identifying and writing initial and final phonemes in consonant-vowel-consonant (CVC) words, e.g. fit, mat, pan; 71-75, 82-84

3 alphabetic and phonic knowledge through:
- sounding and naming each letter of the alphabet in lower and upper case: Activity sheets 15-22
- writing letters in response to letter names: Activity sheets 21-22
- understanding alphabetical order through alphabet books, rhymes and songs: Activity sheets 21-25

4 to link sound and spelling patterns by:
- using knowledge of rhyme to identify families of rhyming CVC words, e.g. hop, top, mop; fat, mat, pat etc.: Activity sheets 71-81
- discrimination onsets from rimes in speech and spelling, e.g. tip, sip, skip, flip, chip: Activity sheets 76-81
- identifying alliteration in known and unknown words: Activity sheets 63-69

Year 1 Term 1

1 from YR, to practise and secure the ability to rhyme, and relate this to spelling patterns through:
- exploring and playing with rhyming patterns: Activity sheets 33-62
- generating rhyming strings e.g. fat, hat, pat: Activity sheets 71-75

2 from YR to practise and secure alphabetical letter knowledge and alphabetical order: Activity sheets 15-25

3 from YR to practise and secure the ability to hear initial and final phonemes in CVC words e.g. fit, mat, pan: Activity sheets 9-10, 71-81, 88-90

4 to discriminate and segment all three phonemes in CVC words: Activity sheets 85-87

5 to blend phonemes to read CVC words in rhyming and non-rhyming sets: Activity sheets 71-81, 88-90

6 to represent in writing the three phonemes in CVC words, spelling them first in rhyming sets, then in non-rhyming sets: Activity sheets 72-75, 78, 81

LISTENING SKILLS

Introduction
This first section of the book is designed to help you develop children's listening skills. Accurate listening is fundamental to the development of literacy. Children need to be able to discriminate and identify sounds with ease, and this, in turn, requires good attention skills. Many teachers report that children enter school with weak listening skills and so it is important to plan classroom activities which will promote the development of these skills.

An essential starting point is frequent listening to stories, rhymes and poems, which should be integral to the early years' classroom curriculum. Encourage the children to be active listeners by asking them questions about the stories. Ensure that the questions you ask are open-ended, requiring more than a one word answer. For example, instead of asking if a character is kind, ask the children what they think about the character. Incorporate sequencing activities into some of these story-telling sessions. This will enable you to check that children are able to tell the main elements of a story in the correct order.

Pay attention to children's responses to oral instructions. Do they follow oral instructions accurately? How many elements of instruction are they able to retain? For example, the following:

"Go to your drawer. Get out your writing book. Take it to your table. Get a pencil. Start your writing." (This contains five elements). Take particular notice if certain children rely heavily on visual cueing. These are the children who tend to do something a little time after everybody else because they watch what other children do and use it as a cue.

The activity sheets in this section are designed as teaching and assessment activities to support the development of accurate listening skills.

TASK 1 — IDENTIFYING SOUNDS
A/S 1

Learning outcomes
- to identify things that make sounds
- to use vocabulary associated with sound: *soft, loud, high, low*

Instructions
Introduce the activity by asking the children to sit in silence for two minutes. Tell them to listen carefully to all the sounds that they can hear around them. At the end of the two minutes get the children to tell you what they heard. Develop their vocabulary by asking them to describe the sound. Was it loud or soft? Was it high or low? Did the sound have a rhythm? Use musical instruments to demonstrate loudness, pitch and rhythm.

Show the activity sheet and talk about the pictures, checking that the children can identify them. Ask the children to tell you which of the things make sounds. Discuss the sounds that the bell, car, girl and bird make. Let the children mimic the sounds. Highlight the fact that some of the things can make different sounds. Focus on the girl and discuss the different noises that children can make: laughing, crying, giggling, talking, shouting, whispering, snoring and so on. Encourage the children to model the noises.

Ask the children how they would know if a car was stationary or how they could tell if it was going fast. Talk about different kinds of bells that the children have encountered. Teach the children the nursery rhyme 'Ding dong bell'. Discuss the different bird sounds that they know: the cock crow, the quacking of ducks and other bird songs. Link this with appropriate nursery rhymes or poems such as 'Cock-a-doodle-do', 'Two little dicky birds' and 'Five little ducks went swimming one day'.

Once the children have completed the activity sheet ask them individually what sounds the things make.

Supporting activities
- Play aural games such as 'Chinese Whispers' and 'Simon says'.
- Talk about different emotions with the children. Show them pictures or photographs portraying different feelings and ask the children what kind of noise the person might make. Select a child to imitate a particular sound and get the other children to identify what emotion the child is exemplifying; for example, if they are laughing they are happy, glad or amused.
- Create a display of children's pictures or paintings of different facial expressions showing different emotions.
- Link the activity sheet to an exploration of different forms of transport. Show the children photographs of different vehicles and discuss the noises that they make. Play a tape of different vehicles' sounds for them to identify.
- Take the children on a listening walk, either in the school or in its vicinity. When the children hear a particular sound they record what they have heard by drawing a picture. When you return to the classroom, discuss all the sounds that they heard and

use this as a basis for a wall display.

Make a tape of sounds in the environment or obtain a tape of sound effects. Include about eight to ten sounds. Sounds could include the following: a car, a dog barking, a clock striking, a playground full of children, a police siren, church bells, an ice-cream van, a motorbike. Play your tape through to the children. When it has finished ask them to draw what they have heard. Observe how many things they can remember. When they have finished, play the tape again to allow them to check for things that they have missed. Pay particular attention to any children who remember less than four sounds. They may have a more general problem with auditory short-term memory. You should observe carefully their responses to other similar tasks which involve short-term memory.

Discuss the sounds that they heard and encourage them to use the appropriate vocabulary: for example loud, soft, high, low and so on.

TASK 2 — DISCRIMINATING SOUNDS
A/S 2

Learning outcomes
- to discriminate between two sounds

Instructions
For this activity you will need the sheet and access to a drum and triangle. Show the children the activity sheet and ask them to name the pictures. Talk about the sounds that the things make and let the children mimic the sounds. Explain that you are going to make one sound out of each pair and that the children will have to identify that sound.

When you are making the sound, hide your mouth behind a screen or a piece of card and ensure that the children concentrate upon listening to the sound. For the drum/triangle pair take both instruments into the classroom and choose one to play behind the screen. As an alternative you could make up a tape of these sounds.

When the children have finished the activity sheet talk about the differences between the sounds that the pairs of objects make using the appropriate vocabulary.

Supporting activities
- Bring some more musical instruments into the classroom. Let the children play with them to learn the sounds that they make and to name the instruments. Choose children to go behind a screen, select an instrument and play for the rest of the group to identify.
- Make a classroom display of different musical instruments incorporating real instruments, photographs, the children's own pictures and information books about music.
- Listen to a range of different musical genres including music from different cultures. Encourage the children to listen carefully to see if they can identify any of the instruments.

TASK 3 — ANIMAL SOUNDS
A/S 3-4

Learning outcomes
- to identify and imitate different animal sounds
- to match words

Instructions
Find pictures of domestic and farm animals. Talk about the animals and the sounds they make. Encourage the children to imitate these sounds. Draw sketches of the animals on a board or a large piece of paper with speech bubbles. Write the animal's sound clearly in the speech bubble. Ask the children to read the words. Ensure that you include a dog, cow, duck and sheep.

Show the children Activity sheet 3, asking them to name the animals and the sounds they make. Introduce Activity sheet 4 with the sketches of the animals you drew before. Get one of the children to find the duck and the word that says 'Quack'. Ask the other children to find that word on their sheet and point to it. Check that all the children have found the correct word. Point out the discriminating features of the word. Once the children have cut out the right speech bubble and stuck it by the duck, let them complete the activity. Keep a careful eye on those children who may have more difficulty matching the words.

Supporting activities
- Teach songs and rhymes that incorporate animal sounds including 'Old MacDonald had a farm', 'This little piggy went to market', 'Baa baa black sheep' and 'Cock-a-doodle-doo'.
- Read the class stories about animals.
- Make a class collage of either a farm or a zoo. Cut out speech bubbles and let the children copy the appropriate sound onto the bubble. Stick the speech bubbles on the collage.
- Use published tapes of animal sounds for the children to listen to and identify.

TASK 4 — RHYTHMIC REFRAINS
A/S 5-6

Learning outcomes
- to learn different refrains from well-known stories
- to recite the refrains with rhythm and intonation
- to use this knowledge to develop one-to-one correspondence with words

Instructions

Many fairy stories have phrases which are repeated frequently during the story. Examples of these refrains include 'Fee fie foe fum' in Jack and the beanstalk, 'Run, run, as fast as you can' in The gingerbread man, 'Little pig, little pig, let me come in' in The three little pigs and 'Trip, trap, trip, trap, over the rickety bridge' in The three billy goats Gruff. The refrains have a strong rhythm and are a useful vehicle for enhancing children's appreciation of rhythm. Many of the refrains also rhyme and can be another way of introducing children to rhyming words.

When you read or share well-known stories which have a refrain running through either encourage the children to join in with you or ask a child or group of children to say it on their own. Enact the story with the children. Act as a model for the children, encouraging them to repeat the phrase with appropriate emphasis and intonation; for example, repeat the giant's refrain from Jack and the beanstalk in a sinister and menacing tone.

Talk about the activity sheets with the children. Ask them to identify the characters in the four pictures in Activity sheet 5. Discuss the stories with the children and let them re-tell each story in the correct sequence. Ask them to tell you what a specific character says in the story; for example "What does the gingerbread man say when he is running away?". Look at Activity sheet 6 with the children. Encourage them to identify which box contains the target refrain. Observe any strategies that the children may use. Some may be able to use their growing sight vocabulary, others might use their knowledge of alliteration; for example recognising the grapheme 'f' in 'Fee, fie, foe, fum'. If a child is unable or reluctant to use any strategy, guide them with the help of careful questioning.

Let the children colour in the pictures on Activity sheet 5 before cutting them out and sticking them by the relevant words. Once the children have stuck in their pictures, ask them to read the refrains to you, pointing at the words as they read. Note whether the children have one-to-one correspondence as they point at the words.

Supporting activities
- Use musical instruments to accompany the children's recitation of the different refrains and to emphasise the rhythm of the words.
- Make a collage or wall picture of one of the stories. Make a speech bubble to write the refrain for the appropriate character.
- Sequence the story with the children. Assign the children different parts of the story to illustrate. Caption the children's drawings, repeating the refrain as often as possible. Make the children's pictures into a class story book or a wall display.
- Encourage the children to listen to pre-recorded tapes of the stories.
- Let the children record their own versions of the stories. Make the children's tapes accessible so that they have the opportunity to listen to them frequently.

TASK 5 — REFRAINS

Learning outcomes
- to learn the refrains from well-known stories
- to recite them with rhythm and intonation

Instructions
Here are the refrains to a number of well-known stories. Read them to the children and ask them to join in when you read them again.

Fee fie foe fum
I smell the blood of an Englishman
Be he alive or be he dead
I'll grind his bones
To make my bread.

Run, run as fast as you can
You can't catch me
I'm the Gingerbread Man!

Little pig, little pig
Let me come in.
Not by the hair of my chinny chin chin!

Who goes trip, trip, trip, trap over the rickety bridge?

Let the children listen to each refrain in turn. Ask them to identify which story each refrain comes from. Encourage the children to use appropriate intonation and rhythm. You could make a tape of the refrains for children to work with on their own.

TASK 6 — LENGTH OF WORDS

Learning outcomes
- to discriminate between long and short words aurally
- to relate this knowledge to printed words

Instructions
Before tackling the activity sheets, you need to start with plenty of aural/oral activities. Say two words, one long and one short, and ask the children which is the longest. If the children find this difficult say the two words emphasising the syllables within the longer word and

saying the shorter word very abruptly. When the children are able to distinguish between long and short words relate this knowledge to the written words. When the children identify the longer word write it up for the children to see and then write the shorter word. Count the number of letters in the two words with the children. Say the words with the children pointing at them as you say them, emphasising the length as you do.

Now show Activity sheet 7 to the children. Check that they are able to identify all the pictures correctly and that they understand the instructions. The words to use for each pair of pictures are : telephone/house, trousers/hat, bee/caterpillar, car/ice-cream, banana/cat, sun/elephant, ship/helicopter, rabbit/pig. Let the children complete the sheet with minimal adult intervention; this will allow you to assess their understanding and knowledge. Once they have completed the sheet ask them to explain some of their choices encouraging them to use appropriate vocabulary: long, short, word and letters.

Present the children with Activity sheet 8. Instruct them to say the names of each of the pictures and to listen carefully before deciding which word relates to which picture. Encourage the children to articulate how they are going to approach the task; they will choose as the longer word either the word that sounds the longer or the one that takes the longer time to say.

Supporting activities
- Provide the children with magazines. Ask them to cut out pictures and to sort the pictures into two sets: 'Long words' and 'Short words'.
- Cut out different words from newspapers and magazines. Choose either very long or very short words. Ask the children to sort the words into two sets. Discuss the words with the children, using the discussion as an opportunity to name letters and explore certain visual features of the words.
- Use the children's own names to develop this exercise. If some children have 'medium-length' names use this as a discussion point with the children. Write the names up to count the letters. Let the children decide whether they are long or short or whether they want to create a new category of 'medium-sized' words.
- Highlight long and short words when you are reading stories with the children.

TASK 7 — PHONEME ACTIVITY
A/S 9-10

Learning outcomes
- to discriminate between similar sounding phonemes

Instructions
Before tackling the activity sheets, you need to start with plenty of aural/oral activities. If possible, gather a collection of pairs of pictures, the names of which differ by only one phoneme (for example mat/bat, cat/cut, bin/bit). Say one of the words and ask the children to point to the relevant picture. Talk about the two words and articulate them clearly, encouraging the children to listen carefully to the difference. Isolate the two different phonemes. Say them to the children. It is vitally important that you pronounce the phonemes carefully and do not distort them; for example 't' not 'ter'. Ask the children to repeat the phonemes. Listen carefully to ensure that the children are saying them correctly. Encourage the children to notice the shape of their mouths when they say the phonemes. Ask them about the position of their tongues when they say the phoneme. Let the children look at their mouths in a small hand mirror when they say the phonemes.

Give the children the activity sheets and ask them to name the pictures. Either that you are going to say one word from each pair which they have to identify and colour. Say the word twice and pronounce it carefully. Here are the words to say:
Activity sheet 9: van, shop, bear, ship, pin
Activity sheet 10: cap, pig, men, bell, pin

Take particular notice of any children who find this task difficult. It may be that they have a difficulty with auditory discrimination; if this is the case they will need plenty of practice with similar activities. It could be that the child has a hearing loss. Approximately ten per cent of primary school aged children have a conductive hearing loss. It is frequently a fluctuating hearing loss and will be more severe if the child has a cold. Monitor any child that you suspect might have a hearing loss carefully and encourage the parents or carers of the child to take the child for a hearing check-up. You will need to be particularly sensitive to any child who does have a hearing difficulty as this could make a significant impact on their acquisition of phonological skills.

Supporting activity
Let the children play with Activity sheets 9 and 10 as phoneme picture pairs cards. One child selects a word to say and the other children indicate which word has been chosen.

Name: _____ Date: _____

Colour the things that make a noise!

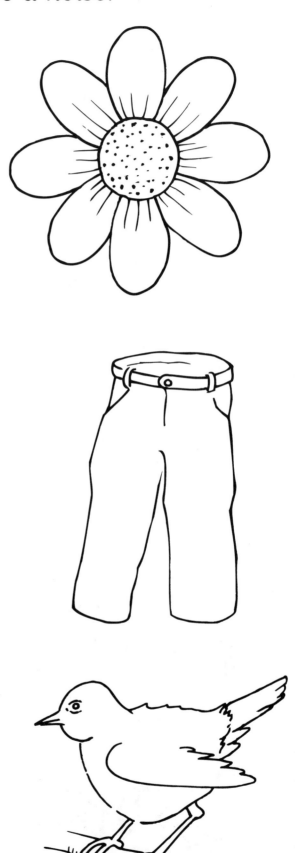

Activity sheet 1

Name: _____ Date: _____

Listen carefully. Colour the one you hear.

Activity sheet 2

Name: _____ Date: _____

What sound do these animals make?

Activity sheet 3

Name: _____ Date: _____

Cut out the speech bubbles.
Stick them with the right animals.

Activity sheet 4

Name: _____   Date: _____

Colour the pictures. Cut them out.
Stick them with the words from the stories.

Activity sheet 5

Name: _____   Date: _____

Fee Fie Foe Fum
I smell the blood
of an Englishman.

Little pig, little pig
Let me come in.
Not by the hair
of my chinny chin, chin.

Run, run as fast as you
can. You can't catch me
I'm the Gingerbread
Man.

Trip, trap, trip, trap
Over the rickety bridge.

Activity sheet 6

Name: _____ Date: _____

Colour the longest word.

Activity sheet 7

Name: _____   Date: _____

Match the pictures with the words.

(cat, caterpillar)	caterpillar cat
(bus, butterfly)	bus butterfly
(aeroplane, ant)	ant aeroplane
(bat, banana)	banana bat
(envelope, egg)	egg envelope

Activity sheet 8

Name: _____   Date: _____

Listen carefully. Colour the one you hear.

Activity sheet 9

Name: _____   Date: _____

Listen carefully. Colour the one you hear.

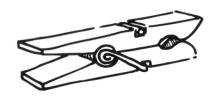 

 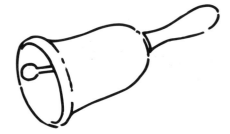

Activity sheet 10

KNOWLEDGE OF LETTERS AND WORDS

Introduction

Children require explicit teaching about features of words and letters. Without such teaching they may remain confused about the difference between letters and words even though they have begun to start reading. It is vital that children begin to use the correct vocabulary to describe the elements connected with reading, for example words and letters.

To young children speech can appear one long flow of sound. As the temporal spaces between spoken words are very short it is hard to distinguish the individual words within a passage of speech. Growing familiarity with print will help the children to identify words, as the spaces between the printed words highlight the discrete nature of words.

As they learn about words the children will need to be taught about the letters that make them up. This knowledge is essential. English is an alphabetical language. It is made up of 26 letters which have two forms: lower case and capital letters. Unlike other objects, the orientation of letters is important to ensure accurate recognition. If you turn a table upside down it remains a table but if you turn a 'b' upside down it changes into a 'p'. Children need extensive exposure to letters to develop accurate and quick recognition.

Marilyn Jager Adams in her acclaimed book *Beginning to read: thinking and learning about print* (1990) reported that the best predictor of children's later reading skills was their knowledge of letters and, specifically, letter names. There has been debate about whether children should be taught letter names or phonemes first. The most recent research would indicate that as well as developing the children's phonological knowledge you should be teaching them the letter names at the same time. Naming objects allows one to conceptualise and remember things, including letters, with greater facility. For example, naming letters allows children to rehearse the spelling of common sight vocabulary.

The activity sheets in this section explore the difference between words and letters, encouraging the children to use the appropriate vocabulary. The sheets also introduce the children to lower case and capital letters and alphabetical order. Knowledge of the alphabet gives the children a framework and is obviously important for many other skills connected with reading. You may wish to introduce the children to the activity sheets concerned with alphabetical order at a slightly later stage. This decision will be based on your assessment of the children's growing competence.

The activity sheets should be supported in the classroom with plenty of activities which allow the children to gain a familiarity with letters and words. They should have ready access to plastic and magnetic letters and the classroom should be a 'word-rich' environment.

TASK 1
A/S 11
LETTERS AND WORDS

Learning outcomes
- to distinguish between words and letters
- to use the correct vocabulary

Instructions

You should take every opportunity to talk about words and letters with the children. This can be done when using big books, asking the children to point out and count either words or letters when looking closely at the text. Ensure that you have a ready supply of different kinds of letters (plastic, magnetic, sponge etc.) in the classroom for the children to play with. Incorporate as many words as you can into the classroom environment and encourage the children to study them carefully.

Introduce the activity sheet by talking about letters and words. Encourage the children to talk about how letters make up words. Talk about the letters in their names. Use an alphabet strip to illustrate your discussion. Look at the activity sheet with the children. Get them to point out the words. There should be some discussion about 'a' and 'I'; if a child does not mention that these could be regarded as either letters or words bring it to their attention. Highlight the fact that the 'I' is a capital letter and that the lower case "i" is not a word. Provide a selection of books and ask the children to find 'a' and 'I' in the texts.

Once the children have completed the basic activity on the sheet, study the sheet with them again. Look carefully at the words. Ask the children if they can read the words and name the letters in them. Count the number of letters in the different words. Get the children to name the individual letters, too, if they can.

Supporting activities

- Display an alphabet strip or chart in the classroom.
- Have a bank of letters available for the children to use.
- Let the children print using sponge letters. They could print their names with the letters. Talk about their work when they have finished, encouraging them to name the letters.

- Make a pack of cards, some with words on, some with letters. These can be used for a simple form of Snap, the children calling "snap" when two letters come up or two words. (The letters and words do not have to match in this game.)

TASK 2 — HOW MANY LETTERS? (A/S 12)

Learning outcomes
- to count the number of letters in a word
- to name the letters

Instructions
Show the children some words written on card. Provide the children with counters and ask them to place a counter on the individual letters. Pay particular attention to the children who find one-to-one correspondence more challenging. Count the counters with the children and ask them how many letters are in the words.

Give out the activity sheet. Ask the children to point out the longest word and the shortest words. Check their suggestions with the children by asking them to count out the letters. Let the children complete the activity sheet. If some children have difficulty counting or creating one-to-one correspondence give them some counters as an additional support. When the children have finished ask them to pass their sheet to a friend to check their answers.

Supporting activities
- Get the children to cut out the words on their sheets and then to sort them into sets: the words with one letter, two letters and so on.
- Give the children a pile of magazines. Ask them to cut out words of their choosing and then to sort them into sets which reflect the different numbers of letters in the words they have chosen.
- Challenge the children to find the longest word that they can in the magazines.
- Ask the children to name the two words in English which only contain one letter. ('a' and 'I')
- Write the children's names on the card. Use this for finding the longest and shortest names and for sorting games.
- Make a simple bar chart to show the number of names of different lengths. Introduce this activity by using counters to illustrate how the bar chart is developed.

Extension learning outcomes
- to read the words on the activity sheet

Instructions
Many of these words are ones that have been identified in the National Literacy Strategy as words that children in the reception class should be able to recognise by sight. Use the activity sheet for assessing the children's knowledge or for reinforcing certain words.

TASK 3 — WORDS AND SENTENCES (A/S 13)

Learning outcomes
- to count the number of words in a short sentence
- to learn the word 'sentence'
- to recognise the significance of full stops
- to use picture cues to read the sentences

Instructions
Use big books to introduce this activity. Share a big book with the children. Choose a page which has a few words on and invite different children up to count the number of words. Reinforce this when sharing books with individual or small groups of children.

Show the children the activity sheet. Look at the first sentence with the children and count the words with them. Read the sentence with the children. Talk about how they know where new words begin, emphasising the importance of the spaces between words. Get the children to put counters on each of the words. Use the word 'sentence' and highlight the capital letter at the beginning of the sentence and the full stop, telling the children that the phrases are 'sentences'.

Let the children complete the activity with minimal intervention but pay particular attention to those children who have difficulty with one-to-one correspondence or with writing numbers. (Some children may benefit from having a number strip to refer to.) Once the children have completed the activity ask them to count out the words with you. Then read the sentences with the children, referring them to the picture cues. As the children read the sentences ask them to point at the words. Observe whether the children are using one-to-one correspondence.

Supporting activities
- If the children have drawn a picture ask them to generate a sentence to describe what they have drawn. Write the sentence on a piece of card. Ensure that you use a full stop. Ask the child to cut the sentence into the individual words. Let them reconstruct the sentence in the correct order.
- Use magazines and ask the children to find sentences with different numbers of words in. Reinforce the concept of the full stop by asking the children how they knew that they were looking at sentences.

- Link these activities with the children's aural appreciation of words within speech. Make up short sentences. Write them on card but do not show the children. Read the sentences to the children and ask them to listen carefully and then to tell you how many words were in the sentence. If they find the task challenging show them the card and point to the words as you say them. Give them strategies by which they can complete the task successfully. Tell them to listen to the whole sentence carefully and to repeat it 'in their head'. As they do so count the words, possibly using their fingers. This strategy of rehearsal is an important one for developing the children's phonological working memory.
- Extend this activity by asking individual children to make up short sentences for the other children to count the number of words in.

TASK 4 — ENVIRONMENTAL PRINT
A/S 14

Learning outcomes
- to identify capital letters in environmental print
- to name the capital letters

Instructions

In English there are two forms of each letters: capitals and lower case. In many classrooms the traditional approach has been to introduce the children to lower case letters first and then to capital letters. This can lead to confusion for the children. Parents frequently introduce their young children to capital letters first and the children are surrounded by environmental print, on signs, posters, advertising hoardings etc., which is often presented in capital letters.

Show the children the activity sheet. Use it as a stimulus for discussion. Talk about what the children can see in the picture and ask them if they can read any of the words. Discuss the kinds of shops that you might find in a street. Point out any that are depicted on the activity sheet. Highlight the significance of the letter 'P' and what it stands for. Ask the children to point to specific letters and name them. Use the words 'lower case' and 'capital'. Tell the children that the signs tend to use capital letters because they are important and want to catch people's attention.

Let the children colour in the picture. Ask them to copy of many of the signs as they can. Talk about the words that the children have copied and ask the children to spell out the words using the correct letter names.

Supporting activities
- Make a classroom display of a street scene. Incorporate as many signs that you can.
- Collect packaging from well-known foodstuffs. Use the packages to discuss the lettering.
- Ask the children to design their own packaging. When they have decided the name of their product get them to write it on using capital letters.
- Incorporate capital letters in labels for the classroom.

TASK 5 — CAPITAL/LOWER CASE LETTERS
A/S 15-17

Learning outcomes
- to be able to distinguish between capital and lower case letters
- to name capital and lower case letters

Instructions

As with other aspects of teaching literacy skills it is important to be explicit and clear when teaching children about capital letters. Tell them that in English, each letter can be written in two ways, either as a capital or as a lower case letter. Use the correct terminology. Terms such as 'big a' or 'little a' will confuse the children: a big 'a' could be a lower case 'a' written in large print. Explain that capital letters are used when things are important; that is why their names begin with capital letters. Use environmental print to demonstrate this: if you want to catch someone's attention you use capital letters.

Before undertaking the activity sheets the children should have had plenty of experience of capital and lower case letters. Provide them with plastic capital and lower case letters and sort them into the two sets. When you are sharing big books with the children talk about the difference between the two forms of letters.

When you present the children with the activity sheets ask the children to name the letters and then to point at either all the lower case or all the capital letters. Once you feel secure that they are able to identify the target group of letters let them complete the activity.

Supporting activities
- Provide the children with a selection of magazines and ask them to cut out letters. Once they have a suitable number of letters get then to sort them into two sets: lower case and capital letters and stick them onto two pieces of paper.
- Use plastic letters and foam letters to reinforce the children's knowledge.

TASK 6 — LOWER CASE AND CAPITAL LETTERS
A/S 18-20

Learning outcomes
- to match lower case and capital letters
- to use the terms 'capital' and 'lower case'
- to name the letters

Instructions
Introduce the activity sheets by presenting the children with a mixture of capital and lower case plastic letters. Ask them to sort them into two sets of capital and lower case letters. Ask the children in turn to choose a lower case letter from the pile and to find the corresponding capital letter. Check that the children can name the letter. Relate the letters that the children have chosen to things with which they are familiar, the beginning of children's names etc.

Draw the children's attention to the physical features of the letters. Highlight letters which have similar features in both capital and lower case forms; for example, 'x' and 'X', 'c' and 'C', and those which have small differences such as 'j' and 'J', 'm' and 'M'. Talk about the differences, that the lower case 'j' has a dot on the top and the capital letter has a bar on the top. Get the children to describe the features of the dissimilar letters, for example 'a' and 'A', 'b' and 'B'. Encourage the children to trace round the plastic letters with their fingers.

Use the activity sheets as an assessment activity. Once you have checked that the children understand the task, let them complete it with minimal adult intervention. When they have finished the tasks ask them to name the letters. Ask them to point to specific letters, for example the lower case 'p'. Arrange the children into pairs and instruct them to ask each other what certain letters are. Listen carefully to ensure that they are using the correct terminology and letter names.

Supporting activities
- Provide the children with large wooden letters and let them trace over them to write their names. Ask them whether they have used capital or lower case letters.
- Put some lower case plastic letters in a bag and some capital letters in another bag. Let the children pull out one lower case letter from the bag. They then have to feel in the other bag to pull out the corresponding capital letter. If they succeed they can keep the pair of letters; if they do not bring out the matching letter both letters go back into the appropriate bag. The winner of the game is the child who has most pairs at the end. (You can alter the difficulty of the game by changing the number of letters you put in the bags at the start of the game.)
- Use lower case and capital letters written on cards to play "pairs" (or pelmanism) with the children.
- Give each child in the group five or six lower case letters. Provide them with magazines and ask them to cut out the corresponding capital letters.
- Write a short sentence or phrase in either lower case or capital letters and ask the children to write under the letters using the other version of the letters.

TASK 7 — WRITE THE ALPHABET
A/S 21-22

Learning outcomes
- to be able to write all the lower case letters of the alphabet
- to be able to recite the alphabet in order

Instructions
These activity sheets will be culmination of much oral and practical work. The National Literacy Strategy advocates the promotion of knowledge of alphabetical order "through alphabet books, rhymes and songs". These should be an integral part of the early years classroom. Display alphabet friezes in the classroom and refer to them constantly, asking children to point to specific letters. Draw the children's attention to the position of the letter in the alphabet : "it's next to ...", "it's near the beginning/middle/end of the alphabet" and so on.

Teach the "alphabet song" to the children. Have a ready supply of letters written on card or plastic letters available. Encourage the children to point to the letters as they sing to allow you to check that they have established one-to-one correspondence. Choose either capital or lower case letters for these activities. Do not mix them.

Use the plastic letters for the children to arrange in alphabetical order. Encourage the children to place them in a horseshoe shape. Once the children have arranged the letters correctly ask them to pick out a specific letter. Get them to tell you which two letters are next to the target letter and where it is in the alphabet. (Ensure that all the children understand the words beginning, middle and end.) Once they have talked about the letter's position ask them to replace it correctly. With more able children use this method to reinforce their spelling of simple cvc (consonant-vowel-consonant) words, encouraging them to notice where they take the letters from and to check that they return the letters to the correct place. With the whole class recite the alphabet, each child saying a letter in turn.

When you present the children with Activity sheet 21, ask them to name all the capital letters before completing the task. You may wish to use Activity sheet 22 as an assessment activity.

Supporting activities
- Let the children cut out the letters on one of the activity sheets, shuffle them and arrange them in the correct order. To add a sense of fun, time the children to see if they can beat their own record.
- Create a class alphabet frieze or alphabet book with the children.

- Stick the children's completed sheets on card and cover with plastic. The children can use them as reference sheets.

TASK 8 — ALPHABETICAL CARS
A/S 23

Learning outcomes
- to arrange letters in alphabetical order

Instructions
Introduce the children to this task by letting them 'play' with plastic letters of all the alphabet and arranging them in alphabetical order. Remove some of the letters so that the children are arranging a limited number of letters in alphabetical order.

When you give the children the activity sheet talk about how cars have letters on them to show which country they come from. Tell the children where the cars depicted on the sheet come from; L - Luxembourg, P - Portugal, I - Italy, B - Belgium, S - Sweden and F - France. Have a map of Europe available to show the children where the countries are.

Once the children have cut out the cars get them to arrange them in alphabetical order for you to check before they stick them on the sheet. (If some children have difficulty with this task let them refer to an alphabet strip as they work.)

Supporting activities
- Distribute different letters of the alphabet to groups of children to arrange in alphabetical order.

TASK 9 — SORTING INTO ORDER
A/S 24

Learning outcomes
- to sort words into alphabetical order

Instructions
Look at the activity sheet carefully with the children. Encourage the children to try to read the names on the shirts. Ask the children to name the first letter of each name. Explain that when you sort names or words into alphabetical order you look at the first letter and use that to determine the order. For the children who encounter more difficulty write the letters on small pieces of card as they name them. Ask the children to sort the letters into alphabetical order before referring again to the names.

Let the children cut out the shirts and order them on the table top before sticking them on the line. This allows you to check that they have understood the task. Allow children to refer to an alphabet strip if necessary.

Supporting activities
- Cut out some shirt shapes. Let the children write their own names on the shirts and decorate them. Make a washing line display in the class for the children to stick their shirts on in alphabetical order.
- When children are lining up, use the opportunity to encourage them to line up in alphabetical order. You will have to teach the children that when you have names which begin with the same letter you have to look at the second letter. Vary this activity by sometimes using the children's surnames.
- Get the children to order their trays in alphabetical order.
- Use cards with selected words from the National Literacy Strategy high frequency words list written on. Ask the children to read the words and then to sort them into alphabetical order.
- Gather together a collection of information books. Look at the indexes with the children. Explain how the indexes are arranged in alphabetical order.

Extension learning outcomes
- to arrange words which begin with the same letter in alphabetical order

Instructions
For children who are able to complete these tasks with ease, challenge them by using words which begin with the same letter so that they have to refer to the second letter.

TASK 10 — ALPHABETICAL ORDER
A/S 25

Learning outcomes
- to sort words into alphabetical order

Instructions
Look at the words on the activity sheet with the children. Ask the children whether the first letter of the words comes near the beginning, middle or end of the alphabet. Take note of the accuracy of the children's responses. Instruct the children to copy the words in alphabetical order in the appropriate sections.

For children who require additional support, give them an alphabet strip to refer to. You may also change the demands of the task by just requiring the words to be written in the correct section but not in alphabetical order.

Name: _____ Date: _____

Colour in the words.

the

y

it

at

z

a

k

look

l

P

Activity sheet 11

Name: _____ Date: _____

How many letters in the words?

cat	☐	the	☐
house	☐	on	☐
am	☐	school	☐
look	☐	a	☐
car	☐	pig	☐
in	☐	I	☐
dog	☐	is	☐

Activity sheet 12

Name: _____   Date: _____

Count the number of words.

I like ice-cream.    ☐

The dog jumped over the gate.    ☐

I saw a pig.    ☐

It's a very big car.    ☐

Look at the house.    ☐

I am happy.    ☐

The ball is blue.    ☐

I like playing with my friends.    ☐

I like reading.   ☐

Activity sheet 13

Name: _____   Date: _____

Activity sheet 14

Name: _____ Date: _____

Colour the lower case letters.

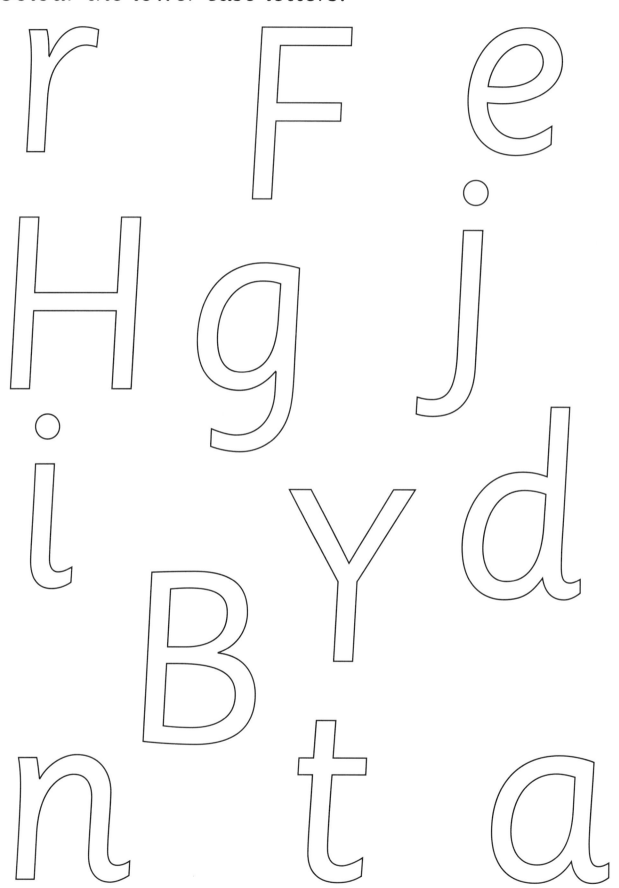

Activity sheet 15

Name: _____ Date: _____

Colour the capital letters.

Activity sheet 16

Name: _____ Date: _____

Colour the capital letters red. Colour the lower case letters blue.

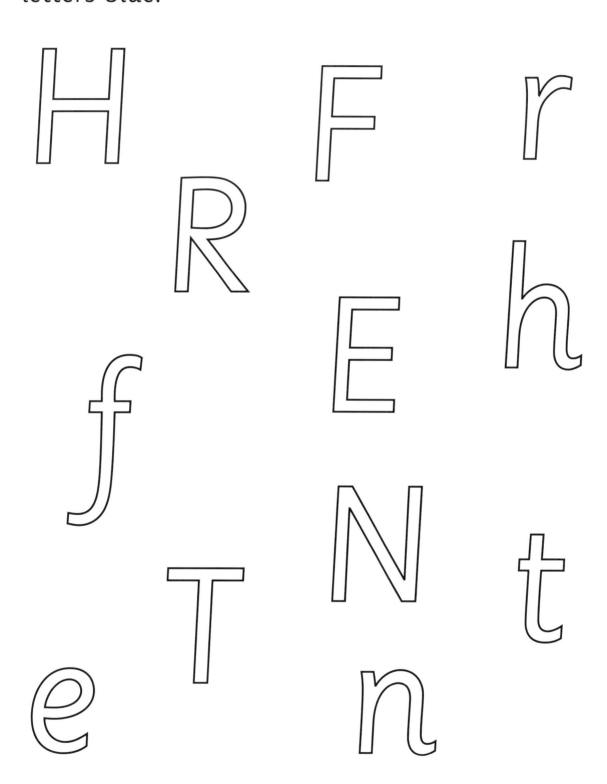

Can you match the capital and lower case letters?

Activity sheet 17

Name: _____ Date: _____

Match the capital and lower case letters.

J i P

    C G
M c W X

      n
j   p
  w l
       g
m   N   x

Activity sheet 18

Name: _____ Date: _____

Match the capital and lower case letters.

s

q

h

S

o

Q

b

H u E

m

M

O

B

e U

Activity sheet 19

Name: _____ Date: _____

Match the capital and lower case letters.

a

l

t

d

V

v

L

A

g

D T

Y

r

y R G

Activity sheet 20

Name: _____ Date: _____

Fill in the lower case letters.

A	B	C	D	E	F	G

H	I	J	K	L	M	N

O	P	Q	R	S	T	U

V	W	X	Y	Z

Activity sheet 21

Name: _____ Date: _____

Fill in the missing letters.

A	B	C		E		
a		c	d		f	g

H	I	J	K			N
h		j		l	m	

O		Q	R	S		
o	p			s	t	u

V	W	X	Y	Z
	w	x		

Activity sheet 22

Name: _____ Date: _____

Cut out the cars. Stick them in alphabetical order.

Activity sheet 23

Name: _____ Date: _____

Cut out the shirts. On a separate piece of paper draw a washing line. Stick the shirts in alphabetical order on your line.

Activity sheet 24

Name: _____ Date: _____

| A–G | N–T |
| H–M | U–Z |

net   hen   banana   log   apple
train   queen   jelly   cat   egg
man   witch   zoo   plum   yacht
umbrella

Activity sheet 25

SYLLABLES

Introduction

The biggest unit of sounds within words are syllables. Syllables are denoted by the beats or internal rhythm of words. Words with one syllable are called monosyllabic; for example house, dog, street. Words with more than syllable are called polysyllabic; for example *ta/ble* (2), *croc/o/dile* (3) and *all/i/ga/tor* (4).

The ability to segment words into syllables is an important strategy in developing effective reading and spelling skills. It allows the reader to be able to break words into more manageable chunks which frequently conform to regular spelling patterns. It is informative to reflect on how you read long unknown scientific words, The most efficient way is to break the word into syllables, decode these and then build the syllables back into the whole word.

As syllables are denoted by beats they can be introduced to the children through plenty of oral work which emphasises the rhythm. This can be complemented by the use of music and, in particular, percussion instruments.

TASK 1 — ONE SYLLABLE OR TWO?
A/S 26

Learning outcomes
- to identify words with one or two syllables

Instructions

There should be plenty of oral work with the children before they are expected to complete the activity sheets. Choose words with different numbers of syllables to say with the children. As you say them emphasise the syllables. Play clapping games with the children clapping on each syllabic beat. Introduce percussion instruments for the children to use on each of the beats. Make up raps or rhythmical phrases using interesting words of different syllabic lengths.

Introduce the activity by showing the children pictures of different animals. Get the children to say the name of each animal and to clap the beats on the syllables. Sort the animals into different sets depending upon the number of syllables in the name.

Show the children the activity sheet and ask them to name the animals. Check that they understand the task. If children require additional support highlight the number 1 in red and the number 2 in blue. Rehearse with the children the strategy that they are going to use: say the word either out loud or sub-vocally and as they do so clap or tap the number of beats. Getting children to articulate the strategy that they use is important in all forms of learning.

Supporting activities
- Let the children think of other animals which have either one or two syllables. Provide the children with books about animals as a reference point.
- Make a classroom display of either a zoo or a farm. Arrange the animals in fields or enclosures depending on the number of syllables in their name.
- Sort other categories, such as transport, furniture and sports, by the number of syllables.

TASK 2 — EQUAL SYLLABLES
A/S 27

Learning outcomes
- to match words with the same number of syllables
- to identify words with 1, 2 or 3 syllables

Instructions

Introduce the activity by showing the children objects or pictures of different syllabic lengths and asking them to sort them. Show the children the activity sheet and get them to name the pictures. As they name the pictures ask them how many syllables are in each word. Observe which strategy, if any, they use. When the children have named all the pictures ask them to point to the objects which have one syllable in their name. Let the children draw a line between the two pictures. The children then complete the activity sheet.

If certain children need more help let them put counters on top of the pictures to indicate how many syllables are in each name before they join the pictures.

TASK 3 — COUNTING SYLLABLES
A/S 28

Learning outcomes
- to identify the number of syllables in their own and others' names

Instructions
Take the opportunity when working with the whole class to explore phonological features of the children's names. Clap their names to illustrate the number of syllables they contain. Sort the children by the syllables in their names: all those with one syllable stand in one corner of the room etc. Play games where you ask all the children with, for example, three syllables to stand up, hop and so on.

Before the children complete the activity sheet ask them who their friends are. Let them rehearse their friends' names out loud, clapping or tapping to determine the number of syllables in the name. When they have drawn the pictures, ask them to name the children in the different sets. Write the children's names under the pictures. You could, if you felt it was appropriate, write the different syllables in different colours. Some children will be able to copy or write the names for themselves.

Supporting activities
- Ask the children to draw a picture of themselves. Let a group take all the finished pictures and sort them by the syllabic length of the children's names before displaying on the classroom wall.
- Make a bar chart with the children of the number of syllables in their names. Each child writes their own name which is then stuck in the appropriate column, 1, 2, 3 syllables etc.
- Let the children draw pictures of their families and write the names underneath the picture. The syllables in each name can be written in a different colour.

TASK 4 — WORDS IN BITS
A/S 29-32

Learning outcomes
- to identify the number of syllables in words

Instructions
Show the children Activity sheet 29 first. Ask them to name the pictures and then to tell you how many syllables are in each word. Introduce Activity sheet 30. Concentrate on the word *bicycle* by asking the children how many syllables they will have to find to make the word. Encourage the children to study the word carefully and then to look for the constituent syllables on Activity sheet 30.

When the children have completed the task ask them again how many syllables are in each word. They should be able to respond to this question with ease.

Let the children complete Activity sheets 31 and 32 with minimal adult intervention. Observe how the children approach the task and their level of understanding.

Supporting activities
- Make syllable jigsaws for the children to complete
- Write long, interesting words in bubble writing. Ask the children to colour in the letters using a different colour for each syllable.

Name: _____ Date: _____

Colour the animals with 1 syllable red.
Colour the animals with 2 syllables blue.

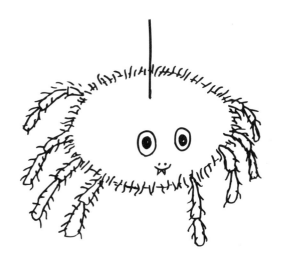

Activity sheet 26

Name: _____ Date: _____

Join the words with the same number of syllables.

flower

house

banana

elephant

book

tortoise

Activity sheet 27

Name: _____ Date: _____

Draw your friends. Sort them by the number of syllables in their names.

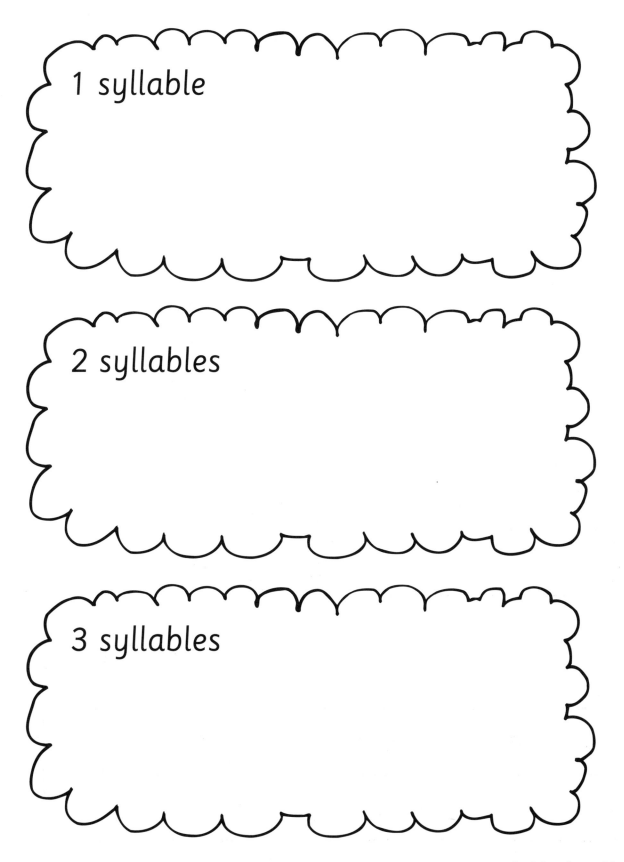

1 syllable

2 syllables

3 syllables

Activity sheet 28

Name: _____ Date: _____

Make the words. Stick on the syllables.

b	i	c	y	c	l	e

t	r	a	i	n

t	a	x	i

a	e	r	o	p	l	a	n	e

Activity sheet 29

Name: _____ Date: _____

Cut out the syllables.

| t | r | a | i | n |

| c | y |

| i |

| o |

| p | l | a | n | e |

| c | l | e |

| a | e | r |

| t | a | x |

| b | i |

Activity sheet 30

Name: _____   Date: _____

Make the words. Stick on the syllables.

e	l	e	p	h	a	n	t

c	a	m	e	l

g	o	a	t

d	i	n	o	s	a	u	r

Activity sheet 31

Name: _____ Date: _____

Cut out the syllables.

| p | h | a | n | t |

| c | a | m |

| e | l |

| n | o |

| e |

| s | a | u | r |

| g | o | a | t |

| d | i |

| e | l |

Activity sheet 32

RHYMES AND RHYMING WORDS

Introduction
One of the most important ways in which young children can develop and enhance their phonological awareness is through their knowledge of nursery rhymes. Nursery rhymes introduce children to the concept of rhyme. Their strong rhythmical structure emphasises the phonological qualities of words. The research work of Bryant and Bradley (1985) demonstrated that children's knowledge of nursery rhymes was a predictor of their later literacy skills.

Nursery rhymes have long been an integral part of the early years' classroom curriculum but were frequently regarded as an incidental fun activity rather than central to the development of literacy skills. It is very important to provide the children with plenty of models which stress the rhythm of the words and to articulate the words clearly so that the children learn the rhymes accurately. Be aware of the children who sit in groups mouthing the words of a rhyme without actually knowing them with any degree of accuracy. Encourage the children to say the rhymes on their own. This allows you to assess their knowledge of different rhymes. Pay particular attention to whether the children use the correct words at the end of lines where words frequently rhyme or share the same rhythm.

The work on nursery rhymes introduces the children to words that rhyme. This is essential for developing an oral appreciation of rimes and onsets. The activity sheets have been designed to teach and reinforce key phonological aspects of nursery rhymes and to develop a secure knowledge of rhyming words.

TASK 1 — A/S 33–37
LEARNING NURSERY RHYMES

Learning outcomes
- to know common nursery rhymes
- to develop memory
- to understand the words 'rhyme' and 'rhythm'

Instructions
The children use the activity sheets to make their own book of nursery rhymes. They can colour the pictures. Read the rhymes to small groups of children. Ask the children to say them to each other. Ask individual children to recite a chosen rhyme to a small group or to the class. Once the children have memorised a rhyme and been able to repeat it from memory, complete the checklist at the back of the book. It is important to introduce the words 'rhyme' and 'rhythm' to the children as they undertake these activities.

Supporting activities
- Ask the children to find other nursery rhymes, poems, jingles and so on to bring into school.
- Make large displays or a frieze for the classroom of their favourite rhymes.
- Allow the children to take their individual books home to show to their parents. Encourage them to say rhymes with their parents.
- Carry out a class survey to find the most popular rhymes.
- Put common nursery rhymes onto tape. Allow the children to listen to the nursery rhymes either in groups or individually. Headphones can be used. Ask the children to draw pictures for the rhymes they have heard.

TASK 2 — A/S 38–39
CHARACTERS AND RHYMES

Learning outcomes
- to recite the nursery rhymes accurately
- to recognise the characters or central features of different nursery rhymes

Instructions
The nursery rhymes pictured on Activity sheet 38 are 'I had a little nut tree', 'Humpty Dumpty', 'Ding dong bell', 'Jack and Jill', 'Mary, Mary, quite contrary' and "Mary had a little lamb'.

The nursery rhymes pictured on sheet 39 are 'Little Jack Horner', 'Old Mother Hubbard', 'Polly put the kettle on', 'Three blind mice', 'Pussy cat, pussy cat' and 'Goosey goosey gander'.

Study each picture with the children, encouraging them to talk about what they can see. Ask them if they can identify any characters in the picture. If they can, ask them to say the relevant nursery rhyme.

After you have talked about the picture tell the children to listen very carefully. Tell them you are going to say a nursery rhyme and when they have heard it they have to colour in the relevant character or feature. Choose and tell a rhyme from one of the sheets. Check that the children have chosen the correct element of the picture to colour. As the children colour encourage them to say the rhyme out loud.

Supporting activities
- The sheets may be used as an assessment tool. Once a child knows the rhymes accurately they can colour in the relevant section. This allows the child to keep their own record of their growing knowledge of nursery rhymes.
- Ensure that your book displays include nursery rhyme books.
- Let the children listen to nursery rhyme and poetry tapes. Encourage them to borrow them to take home.
- Incorporate a rich diet of nursery rhymes and poetry in the daily curriculum. Take every opportunity to use rhyme and poetry, encouraging the children to say the verses accurately with clear articulation, expression and rhythm.
- Nursery rhymes can be used to reinforce other curriculum areas. Below are listed relevant nursery rhymes for common themes in the early years' curriculum.

Food: Little Tommy Tucker; Little Miss Muffett; This little pig went to market; Pat-a-cake, pat-a-cake; Betty Botter; Half a pound of tuppeny rice; Pease porridge hot; Simple Simon; Diddle diddle dumpling; Sing a song of sixpence; Jack Sprat; Georgie Porgie; Little Jack Horner; Old Mother Hubbard; Peter, Peter, pumpkin eater; The Queen of Hearts; Polly put the kettle on.

Animals: Little Boy Blue; Little Bo Peep; Ding dong bell; Tom, Tom, the piper's son; Baa, baa, black sheep; Mary had a little lamb; Goosey, goosey gander; Old Mother Hubbard; Hickory, dickory, dock; Hickety, pickety, my black hen; The four and twenty sailors; This is the house that Jack built; The three little kittens; Higglety, pigglety, pop!; Three young rats; Cock a doodle doo!

Weather: One misty moisty morning; It's raining, it's pouring; Here we go round the mulberry bush; The North Wind doth blow; Dr Foster.

Flowers and plants: Mary, Mary; Ring-a-ring-a-roses; I had a little nut tree.

Transport: Yankee Doodle; Bobby Shaftoe; I saw a ship a-sailing; The four and twenty sailors.

Music: Hey diddle diddle; Old King Cole; Ride a cock horse.

Extension learning outcomes
- to identify and generate rhyming words

Instructions
With the children who have a good knowledge of nursery rhymes focus on the rhyming words in certain nursery rhymes portrayed in the pictures. For example on Activity sheet 38 look at the picture prompt for 'Ding Dong Bell'.

Get the children to recite the nursery rhyme. Repeat it to the children putting emphasis on the words 'bell' and 'well' as you say it. Tell the children that these words rhyme because they have the same sound at the end of the word: 'ell'. Ask the children to colour in the bell and well. Talk about other words that rhyme with 'bell', encouraging the children to suggest correctly rhyming words. Repeat this with the picture prompt for 'Jack and Jill' on Activity sheet 38. The same activity may be repeated for 'Jack Horner' (Horner/corner) and 'Old Mother Hubbard' (Hubbard/cupboard) on sheet 39.

Talk about the other nursery rhymes portrayed in the picture. Chant them with the children, asking them to identify the rhyming words and encouraging them to think of other words in the same rhyming family.

Supporting activity
- Record versions of the rhymes on sheets 38-39 onto a tape. This can be used in a flexible way either for teaching the children the nursery rhymes or as a stimulus for colouring in relevant parts of the picture.

TASK 3 — SEQUENCING RHYMES (A/S 40-41)

Learning outcomes
- to repeat the nursery rhymes accurately
- to sequence the nursery rhymes using picture clues

Instructions
Rehearse the target nursery rhyme (either 'Jack and Jill' or 'Wee Willie Winkie') with the children. As 'Wee Willie Winkie' is less well-known you may have to teach it to the children. Check that the children have an accurate knowledge of the rhyme and that they understand the vocabulary; for example 'pail', 'crown', 'rapping', 'nightgown'. Get the children to cut out the strips. Look at the strips with the children. Discuss what is happening in the picture and encourage them to predict what the text might say. Ask them to sort the pictures into the correct order and to read the nursery rhyme to you. Let them point at the words as they say the rhyme. The strips may then either be stapled together to make a strip book or stuck onto a piece of paper for the children to keep and refer to. (If you want the children to colour the pictures young children will find it easier to colour them before they cut them into strips.)

Supporting activities
- Make a collection of the children's favourite nursery rhymes in a big book with each child illustrating a different rhyme.
- Record a class cassette with the children to accompany the big book. Make this available for them to listen to. Encourage them to use headphones for careful listening.

- Choose different rhymes from 'Jack and Jill' and 'Wee Willie Winkie'. Write each line on a big piece of paper. Ask children to illustrate their line and then to work together to put the rhyme in the correct sequence. Display the nursery rhyme on the wall.

Extension learning outcomes
- to notice the spelling patterns of the words that rhyme

Instructions
Ask the children who are developing a secure understanding of rhyme to underline the words at the end of each line. Encourage them to study the letters in the words carefully, naming them out loud. Get them to tell you if they notice anything about the letter patterns (in other words, the shared rimes).

Ask the children to think of other words in the same rhyming family. Write them for the children to see or make them with plastic letters.

Put 'Wee Willie Winkie' onto tape for children to learn.

TASK 4 **CHANGING NURSERY RHYMES**
A/S 42-43

Learning outcomes
- to generate rhyming words

Instructions
Get the children to repeat the conventional version of the nursery rhyme 'Humpty Dumpty'. Emphasise the words 'wall' and 'fall'. Check that the children understand that these are rhyming words. Talk about other words in that family: tall, call, ball, hall etc.

Read the first adapted version of 'Humpty Dumpty' with the children. Ask them what the missing word could be and when they have made an appropriate suggestion reinforce the shared sound pattern with the children. After they have drawn their picture talk about other words that rhyme with 'car'. Read the next two adaptations with the children checking that the words they suggest rhyme before they draw the pictures. On Activity sheet 43 there is more than one possibility for the rhyme of 'chair': bear, fair, hare, mare, pear, tear. Accept all these suggestions as we are concentrating upon the shared sounds, phonemes. The differences in written patterns (graphemes) do not matter at this stage.

Supporting activities
- Play aural games with the children changing other nursery rhymes: 'Old Mother Sable went to the ...', 'Old Mother Fox went to her ...', 'Old Mother Slade tripped over her...', 'Old Mother Bell fell down a ...', 'Little Jack Blair sat on a ...' etc.

Extension learning outcomes
- to identify the shared spelling pattern
- to generate a shared spelling pattern

Instructions
For children who are developing an understanding of the relationship between the sound qualities and the written representation of words use sheet 42 to develop this further. Write the words 'car' and 'star' by the pictures. Encourage the children to study the words carefully saying the letter names. Ask them what they notice about the words. Repeat this with 'floor' and 'door'. In the third section write 'house' and just a 'm' by the mouse. Observe if the children are able to complete the word.

TASK 5 **RHYMING WORDS**
A/S 44-52

Learning outcomes
- to be able to match rhyming words
- to generate rhyming words

Instructions
The nine activity sheets can be used in several ways to achieve the learning outcomes.

Choose one of the sheets of rhyming word pairs (44-47). Ensure that the children know the names of all the objects by asking them to name each of the pictures. When the children have cut out the pictures ask them to sort the pictures into pairs of words that rhyme. (Check that the children understand that word 'rhyme' means having the same sound at the end of the word.) Let the children stick their rhyming pairs on the prepared grid on Activity sheet 48. Put the children in small groups and ask them to think of other words that rhyme with the target words. Bring the children together in a bigger group (or the whole class) to share all the words that they have thought of. The children can then repeat the activity using a different rhyming word sheet.

Either photocopy the sheets (44-47 inclusive) onto card or cut out all the pictures and mount them on card. These pictures can be used to play a number of games to reinforce the learning outcomes, as follows:

Pelmanism Use the pictures from sheets 44, 45 and 46 for this game. Organise the children into a small group (three or four children). Check that the children name all the pictures correctly before starting the game. Shuffle the pictures and turn them face down on the floor or table top. The children take it in turn to turn two pictures over. If they find a rhyming pair they keep the cards and have another go. If their cards do not rhyme they return the cards, face down, to the same place. The winner is the child who has the most pairs when all the cards have been matched. Ask the children to think of other words that rhyme with their pairs. Train the children to play this game with minimal adult supervision.

Snap (Use cards from sheets 44, 45, 46 and 47 for this.) The children play this game with a partner. Deal out all the cards to the two children. Teach them how to turn over one card at a time simultaneously. If the pictures on the two cards rhyme the children say "snap". The first child to say snap keeps the cards and adds them to their pile. The winner is the child who eventually gets all the cards or has the most cards after a pre-determined time. Encourage the children to say the two rhyming words before they pick up. This reinforces the concept of rhyme. Ask them if they can think of any other word that rhymes with their pair.

Bingo Photocopy Activity sheets 49-52 onto card or stick the photocopies on card. Use with the cards from sheets 44, 45, 46, and 47. Four children may play the game at any time. Each child has a bingo sheet. Ask the children to name all the pictures on their bingo card before the game starts. Place the pile of cards in the centre of the table. Turn over one card at a time. If a child believes that the name of the picture rhymes with one on their card they indicate in a pre-determined way (for example putting up their hand or saying "rhyme"). The first child to make the sign covers the relevant picture on their sheet with the card. You can reinforce the rhyming link by requiring the children to say "... rhymes with ..." before they claim the card. The winner is the first child to cover all the pictures on their sheet. Make it clear to the children at the beginning of the game that they cannot claim identical pictures.

Extension learning outcomes
- to identify shared spelling patterns of rimes

Instructions
If some children have a secure understanding of the concept, extend the activity by writing the words by the picture. Get the children to read the words and to spell out the words using letter names. Ask them if they notice anything about the words: that they share the same letters at the end of the word. For children who are beginning to appreciate the relationship between sounds and print, write down the word for one of the pairs and let the child try to write the name of the other noun.

TASK 6 — MATCHING RHYMES
A/S 53-55

Learning outcomes
- to match rhyming words aurally/orally

Instructions
Ask the children to cut out the numbers from the activity sheets and stick each one under the rhyming picture. It is important to ensure that the children are able to recognise numbers if they are to undertake this activity.

Supporting activities
- Using plain paper cut out very large numbers and mount on the wall. Ask the children to find pictures or draw pictures of things that rhyme with the numbers to stick on each number.
- Sing and say number rhymes 'This Old Man', 'One, two, buckle my shoe', 'One, two, three, four, five, once I caught a fish alive' etc.
- Use Activity sheet 55 to play this game for two. A dice is needed. Each child throws the dice in turn. They may move the number of stepping stones shown by the dice if they can think of a word that rhymes with the number.

TASK 7 — RHYMING I SPY
A/S 56

Learning outcomes
- to identify words which rhyme

Instructions
Introduce the activity by playing 'Rhyming I Spy' orally with the children. Choose an object in the classroom and say "I spy with my little eye something that rhymes with ... " (for example 'bear'). Read the activity sheet with the children and check that they are able to name the pictures accurately. When they have completed the sheet ask them to read it to you with the rhyming word they have identified.

Extension learning outcomes
- to generate rhyming words

Instructions
Choose one of the other pictures (for example 'ball') and ask the children to think of words that rhyme with that word. Incorporate the 'I Spy' game as a regular classroom activity, letting the children ask the question. You could sometimes let the children make up nonsense words as the trigger word (for example 'pindow'). Such games are good for enhancing the children's phonological awareness and sophistication.

Supporting activity
- Tell the children that you are going to play 'Rhyming I Spy' again but this time they are going to draw their answers. Encourage the children to think of more than one answer. Say each I Spy twice. Here are some

suggestions:
I spy with my little eye something that rhymes with tree.
I spy with my little eye something that rhymes with wall.
I spy with my little eye something that rhymes with mouse.
I spy with my little eye something that rhymes with rain.
I spy with my little eye something that rhymes with hair.

TASK 8 — ODD ONE OUT
A/S 57

Learning outcomes
- to be able to discriminate words that rhyme
- to be able to generate rhymes

Instructions
Introduce the activity by showing the children four objects or pictures, three of which rhyme and one that doesn't. Get the children to name the objects in chorus. Ask one child to sort the objects into a set of those that rhyme. Show the children that there is one object left out. Let them repeat the names of the object to reinforce the concept. When you give the children the activity sheet ask them to name all the objects before they start. Pay particular attention to the words that may be unfamiliar to the children, such as 'fan', and those that might be confused with other words, for example 'rug' not 'mat'. Check that they understand what they have to do. Talk to them when they have finished, asking them to articulate why they have made the choices that they have.

Extend the activity by writing the names of the pictures underneath. Get the children to study the words carefully and ask them to notice any differences they can between the word that does not rhyme and those that do. Encourage them to talk specifically about the letter patterns. With children who are developing a good appreciation of rhyme and its connection with print, write the name of one of the rhyming triplets and encourage them to try to write the names of the other two rhyming words.

Supporting activity
- Here is another version of the game, in which the children have to draw the answer. Tell the children to listen carefully and to draw a picture of the word that does not rhyme. Here is a list of words to use. Read each set twice.
  Jock lost his ...
  Meg hurt her ...
  Mick tripped over a ...
  Molly licked her ...
  Roy broke his ...
  Dale saw a ...

TASK 9 — MATCHING RHYMES
A/S 58-60

Learning outcomes
- to match rhyming words orally/aurally

Instructions
Ask the children to cut out each puppet, colour the puppet and the stick. Tell them the name of each puppet and ask them if they can think of any words that rhyme with each name. Ask the children to cut out the pictures on Activity sheet 60. These should be spread out over a desk. Talk to the children about the names of the pictures and ensure that they are quite clear what each picture represents. Four children are each given a puppet and must collect the pictures that rhyme with the name of their puppet.

Supporting activities
- Ask the children to look around the room and make collections of actual objects that rhyme with the name of their puppet. Make a display of the objects with the puppets.
- Ask the children to draw their collection. They could make a book of rhyming pictures.
- Ask the children to complete the sentences:
  Kate likes to ...? (skate)
  Dan has a ...? (pan, fan)
  Pat sits on the ...? (mat)
  Ted goes to ...? (bed)

  Further sentences can easily be generated. Encourage the children to make up their own sentences for others to complete.

- Ask the children to make more puppets and give them different names. They need to be names that will rhyme relatively easily with familiar items/pictures. Suggested names: Mick, Paul, Meg, Sam, Kim, Mum, Roy, Billy, Molly, Tess, Dale, Jock, Jade, Jack, Ben.

Extension learning outcomes
- to write words that rhyme with the names of the puppets using analogy

Instructions
Ask the children to record the names of the puppets they have made. They should write them at the top of a piece of paper so they can write further rhyming words in a column underneath. Ask the children to underline the rime element in each word.

TASK 10 **A/S** 61-62

RHYME GENERATION ACTIVITY

Learning outcomes
- to generate rhyming words independently

Instructions
This is an excellent assessment activity to ensure the children are familiar with rhyme and are able to provide rhyming words easily. Check that the children know the name of each item. The children draw a rhyming picture in the space provided.

Supporting activities
- Children make up rhyming couplets; these could be based on their own or made up names, names of their pets etc., for example My dog Sid sleeps in a lid., The snake slid over a rake etc. The children can illustrate these or make a big book for the classroom, with a rhyme on each page along with an illustration.
- Invent a password to enter the classroom. As the children come in, they must provide a rhyming word. Encourage the children to make up nonsense words (as long as they rhyme) for this activity.
- Practise generating rhyming words. Provide the children with a piece of paper divided into six rectangles. Ask the children to draw a picture of something that rhymes with a word you read out. Read each word twice and encourage the children to come up with as many words as they can. Here are six words to rhyme with: star, head, ship, bone, chair, lock.

Name: _____ Date: _____

Baa, baa, black sheep, have you any wool?

Yes, sir,
Yes sir,
three bags full;

One for the master, and one for the dame,

And one for the little boy who lives down the lane.

Little Bo Peep, she lost her sheep,

And couldn't tell where to find them;

Leave them alone and they'll come home,

Bringing their tails behind them.

Activity sheet 33

Name: _____ Date: _____

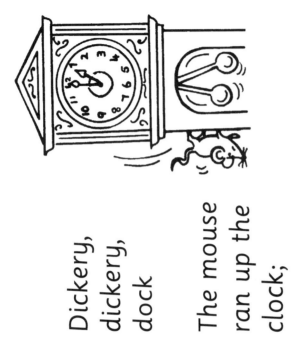

Dickery, dickery, dock

The mouse ran up the clock;

The clock struck one,
The mouse ran down,

Dickery, dickery, dock.

Higgledy, Piggledy, my black hen,

She lays eggs for gentlemen;

Sometimes nine, and sometimes ten

Higgledy, Piggledy, my black hen.

Name: _____   Date: _____

Lady-bird, Lady-bird,
fly away home,

The house is on fire, the children have gone;

All but one, and her name is Ann,

And she crept under the frying pan.

One, Two, Three, Four, Five,

Once I caught a fish alive.

Why did you let it go?

Because it bit my finger so.

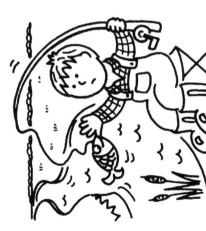

Activity sheet 35

Name: _____   Date: _____

I can say these nursery rhymes by myself:

Jack and Jill
Dickory dock
Little Bo Peep
Baa, Baa, Black Sheep
I had a little Nut Tree

Jack and Jill went up the hill

To fetch a pail of water;

Jack fell down and broke his crown,

And Jill came tumbling after.

Up Jack got and home did trot,

As fast as he could caper;

And went to bed
to mend his
head

With
vinegar
and
brown
paper.

Name: _____ Date: _____

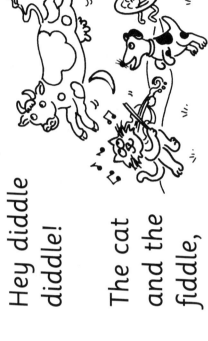

Hey diddle diddle!

The cat and the fiddle,

The cow jumped over the moon;

The little dog laughed

to see such sport

And the dish ran away with the spoon.

I had a little nut tree,

And nothing would it bear

But a silver apple

And a golden pear;

The king of Spain's daughter

came to visit me,

All for the sake of my little nut tree.

Activity sheet 37

Name: _____   Date: _____

Activity sheet 38

Name: _____ Date: _____

Activity sheet 39

Name: _____ Date: _____

Jack fell down

Went up the hill

And Jill came tumbling after

Jack and Jill

And broke his crown

To fetch a pail of water

Name: _____ Date: _____

Rapping at the window, crying through the lock

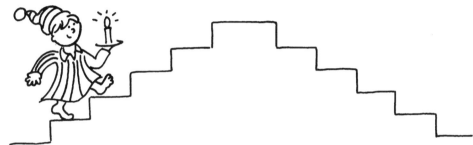

Upstairs and downstairs in his nightgown

Are the children all in bed? – for now it's eight o'clock

Wee Willie Winkie runs through the town

Activity sheet 41

Name: _____ Date: _____

Draw a picture to make the rhyme.

- sat in his 🚗

- saw a bright ☐

- sat on the 🧱

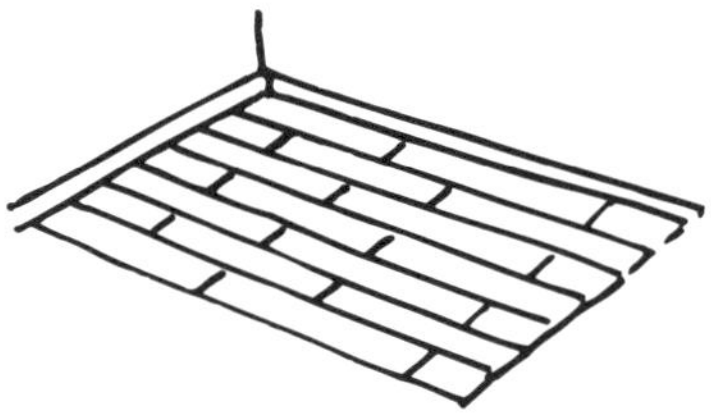

- opened the ☐

- sat by the 🏠

- saw a brown ☐

Activity sheet 42

Name: _____ Date: _____

Draw a picture to make the rhyme.

sat on a 🪑

saw a big

---

sat by the 🌊

was stung by a

---

sat in the 🌧️

saw a jet

Activity sheet 43

Name: _____   Date: _____

Cut out the pictures.

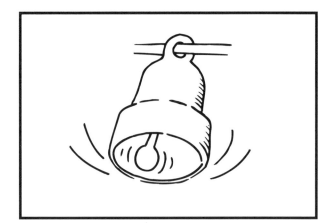

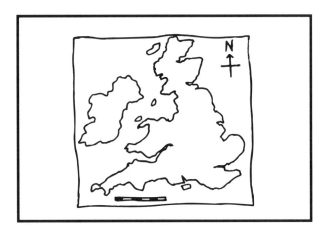

Activity sheet 44

Name: _____ Date: _____

Cut out the pictures.

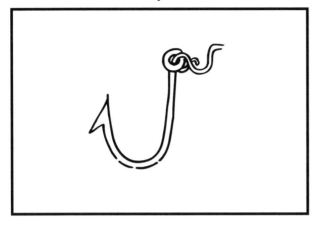

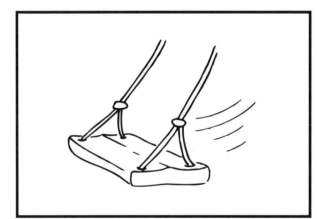
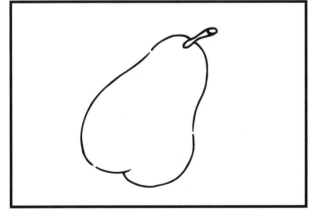

Activity sheet 45

Name: _____   Date: _____

Cut out the pictures.

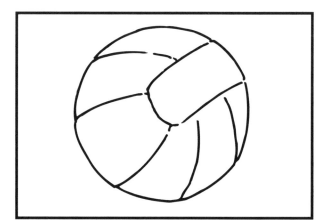

Activity sheet 46

Name: _____ Date: _____

Cut out the pictures.

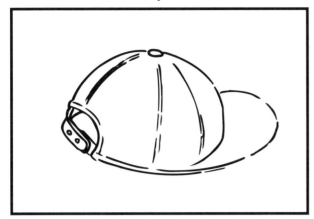
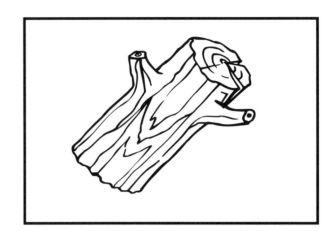

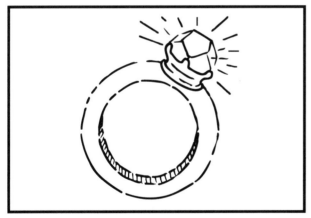

Activity sheet 47

Name: _____   Date: _____

Stick the rhyming pairs together.

Activity sheet 48

Name: _____ Date: _____

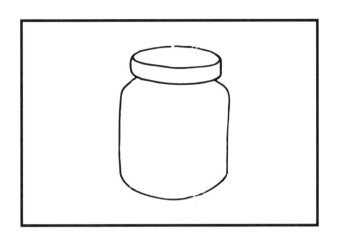 

 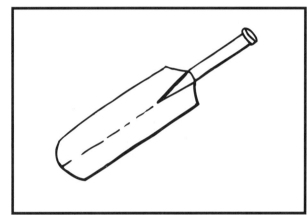

Activity sheet 49

Name: _____ Date: _____

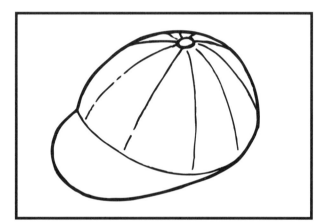
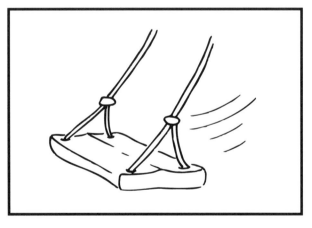
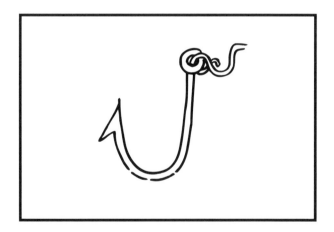
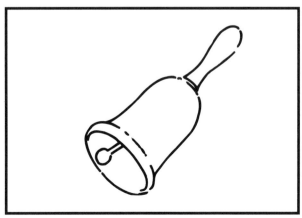

Activity sheet 50

Name: _____ Date: _____

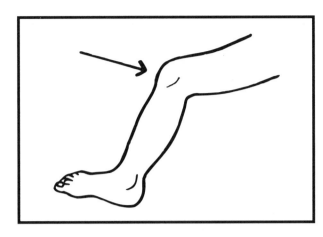 

 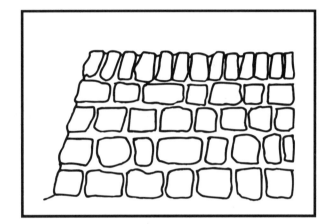

Activity sheet 51

Name: _____ Date: _____

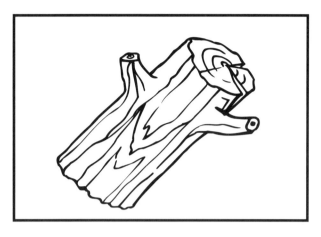
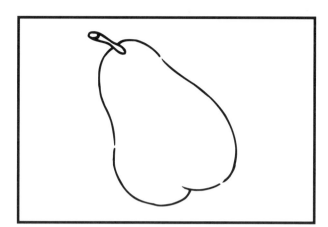

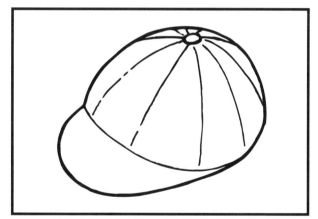

Activity sheet 52

Name: _____ Date: _____

Stick the numbers by the rhyming pictures.

Activity sheet 53

Name: _____ Date: _____

Stick the numbers by the rhyming pictures.

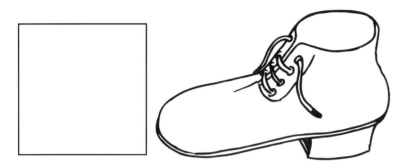

11

Activity sheet 54

Name: _____ Date: _____

Cut out the numbers.

1	2
3	4
5	6
7	8
9	10

Activity sheet 55

Name: _____ Date: _____

I spy with my little eye
something that rhymes with   Colour it.

   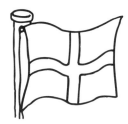

I spy with my little eye
something that rhymes with   Colour it.

I spy with my little eye
something that rhymes with   Colour it.

I spy with my little eye
something that rhymes with   Colour it.

Activity sheet 56

Name: _____ Date: _____

Say the names of the pictures.
Colour in the picture that doesn't rhyme.

Activity sheet 57

Name: _____   Date: _____

Activity sheet 58

Name: _____ Date: _____

Activity sheet 59

Name: _____ Date: _____

Cut out the pictures.

Activity sheet 60

Name: _____ Date: _____

Activity sheet 61

Name: _____ Date: _____

Activity sheet 62

ALLITERATION

Introduction
This section introduces children to listening carefully to the phonemes at the beginning of words. If the children are going to use initial phonemes for both early spelling attempts and cues in their reading it is most important that they develop an awareness of these phonemes and the ability to both match and generate them for themselves.

This is primarily a listening and speaking activity and graphemes are not being introduced in this section. Some children have more difficulty than others in hearing the fine differences between phonemes and need plenty of practice at this skill. The activity sheets build on the previous work on listening skills.

It is important to note any pupils that find this particularly difficult. They may have some problem with acuity or it may be a perceptual problem and therefore require further practice in this skill. The sheets are useful for both teaching and as assessment material.

TASK 1 — ALLITERATION — A/S 63-67

Learning outcomes
- to match phonemes at the beginning of words
- to understand and use the word 'phoneme'

Instructions for Activity sheet 63
Ask the children to look at the picture of the sea-shore. Talk to them about their own experiences of visiting the sea-side. Ask them about the activities they enjoy at the sea-side and about all the things they are likely to see. Ask the children to list all the items that can see in the picture that start with the phoneme 's' (as at the beginning of 'sun'). The children can colour these items in the picture and add any further items that begin with the same phoneme. Take the opportunity when talking about the picture to introduce the word 'phoneme' and ensure they understand that it means a single sound.

Instructions for Activity sheet 64
Look at the picture with the children. Ask them to name as many items as possible. Ensure they use the correct words. Ask the children to find as many items as they can, starting with the phoneme 'c' (as in 'cat'). Ask them to draw the items in the space provided. They can add their own ideas to the picture if they can think of more items beginning with the same phoneme.

Instructions for Activity sheet 65
Ask the children to draw a line to join the pictures that start with the same phoneme. Ensure that the children know what each picture represents by naming them first and ask the children to name all the pictures before they begin.

Instructions for Activity sheet 66
Ask the children to colour the pictures that start with the same phoneme as the first picture. Ask the children to name the pictures before they begin.

Instructions for Activity sheet 67
Ask the children to colour the pictures with a colour whose name starts with the same phoneme, for example penguin - purple or pink, grass - green, bird - black or brown, yacht - yellow, blanket - blue or black, roof - red.

Supporting activities
- Use other pictures from story or non-fiction books that have a number of words that start with the same sound for the same activity.
- Ask the children to make their own pictures including as many items starting with a particular phoneme. They could use pictures cut from magazines to make collage pictures.
- Make a very large picture for the classroom wall and ask each child to add a picture that starts with a particular phoneme e.g. a busy street market: pears, plums, potatoes, puppies, paper bags, pictures, packing cases, packages, pails, people, pots, pans peaches etc.; a playground or garden: balls, bicycles, balloons, bat, beech tree, birds, butterfly, blossom, boy, branch, bricks, buggy, bumblebee, bush etc.
- Read a story that has several words beginning with the same phoneme; ask the children to put up their hand or indicate in some other way when they hear the target phoneme.

TASK 2 — STORY PHONEMES

Learning outcomes
- to detect the same phoneme within continuous text

Instructions

Provide each child with some counters and a small plastic pot or other container. Read this story through slowly to the children once:

Betty and Billy were hungry. So they decided to make some bread. They went to the kitchen and got a bowl. They mixed the flour and water and made a big ball of dough. Next they rubbed a baking tin with butter so the dough wouldn't stick. They lit the oven and put the tin inside. Soon came one of the best bits - a wonderful smell coming from the oven. At last the bread was ready. Taking care not to burn their hands they turned over the tin and out came the bread. Delicious!

Now explain that you are going to read the story through again. This time ask the children to place a counter in the pot every time they hear a word that begins with the phoneme 'b'. At the end ask them to compare the number of counters in the pot with a friend. (There are 13 words that start with 'b' in all.) You could put the stories on tape and get the children to work independently. Ask them to listen to the tape again to check their answer.

TASK 3 — MAKING ALLITERATIONS
A/S 68-69

Learning outcomes
- to generate alliterative phonemes

Instructions for Activity sheet 68

This is a further development of children's ability in using individual phonemes. The children are asked to generate their own words to match a cue word or phrase. As the children are not writing any graphemes at this stage it is perfectly acceptable if they use words that have the same phoneme at the beginning of the word but are represented by different graphemes, e.g. Christmas, kick, feather, pheasant etc.

Read the words under each picture to the children. Emphasise the first phoneme. Ask the children to draw their own picture using first their own name and then a friend's name and adding an alliterative verb. Children will need a simple explanation of what a verb is and may need help in generating 'doing words'. Here are some suggestions for the whole alphabet: angling, bowling, crawling, dancing, etching, finding, gardening, hurting, illustrating, joking, kicking, licking, mending, knitting, opening, playing, queuing, racing, standing, taping, undoing, vanishing, waving, yawning, zigzagging.

Instructions for Activity sheet 69

Ask the children to draw more pictures beginning with the same phoneme as the ones illustrated. Ask them to colour their pictures.

Supporting activities
- Make a collection of real objects that start with the same phoneme. Children will often have small toys that they can bring in to add to the collection. Here are some sets of words for alliterative work that can be illustrated or represented by objects.

bed	hen	pig	cup	dog	fat
bus	hand	pen	cat	dig	fox
box	hat	pan	cap	duck	foot
bag	house	pipe	car	doll	fire
bell	horse	pond	cow	door	

girl	jug	king	log	man	nut
gate	jar	kite	leg	moon	net
goat	jumper	key	lion	map	nest
gun	jam	kangaroo	leaf	milk	nail

rat	sun	tap	window
rabbit	sock	tent	wall
ring	saw	table	web
roof	sack	ten	watch

- Ask the children to think of something they own (or would like to own) that starts with the same phoneme as their name e.g. William's wellingtons, Janet's jigsaw, etc. Make a collection to produce a class booklet or make a large display for the classroom wall.
- Play 'I Spy' with the children.
- Play 'I packed my bag'. Start the activity by saying "I packed my bag with a .... sweet". The children take turns to repeat the sentence but each time add another item which must start with the same phoneme e.g. "I packed my bag with a sweet, a Sindy doll, a silver bracelet, a saucer etc.".
- Draw very large bags and ask the children to draw all the items they have thought of during the game inside each bag.

TASK 4 — TONGUE TWISTERS
A/S 70

Learning outcomes
- to hear alliterative phonemes

Instructions

Tongue twisters are an excellent way of developing children's articulation skills and allowing them to feel how certain phonemes are made. It is also a fun activity that children enjoy. They will happily make up their own tongue twisters. Ask the children to colour the lorries red and yellow alternatively. Ask them to say "Red lorry, yellow lorry, red lorry" as quickly as they can.

Supporting activities
- Teach the children other tongue twisters and ask them to say as quickly as possible e.g. 'Peter Piper picked a peck of pickled peppers' etc. Ask the children to make up their own tongue twisters and ask them to say them to each other. A class book, with illustrations, can be made of their ideas.

Name: _____ Date: _____

Activity sheet 63

Name: _____ Date: _____

Draw the pictures that start with the same sound as 🍵

Activity sheet 64

Name: _____ Date: _____

Join the pictures that start with the same sound.

 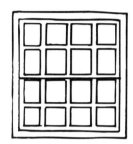 

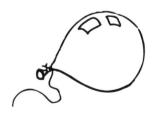  

Activity sheet 65

Name: _____ Date: _____

Colour the pictures that start with the same sound as the first picture.

Activity sheet 66

Name: _____ Date: _____

Colour the pictures using a colour that start with the same sound.

Activity sheet 67

Name: _____   Date: _____

	Draw yourself
 Fiona fishing	
 Ben biking	Draw a friend

Activity sheet 68

Name: _____   Date: _____

Draw some more pictures for Ted.

Draw some more pictures for Ben.

Activity sheet 69

Name: _____ Date: _____

Red lorry, yellow lorry, red lorry, yellow lorry…
Say it as quickly as you can.

Colour red

Colour yellow

yellow

red

red

yellow

Activity sheet 70

ONSET AND RIME

Introduction
Research has shown that young children find it relatively easy to segment words into syllables and the onset and rime and may do this spontaneously (Bradley and Bryant - 1985, Goswami - 1995). The onset is any consonant phonemes which precede the vowel and the rime is the portion of the syllable which includes the vowel phoneme and any consonants following it. For example:

Onsets	Rimes
c	at
bl	ack
str	ing
sh	ip

It appears that the division into onset and rime is developmentally between the ability to hear syllables and the considerably more difficult task of being able to use individual phonemes for word attack and spelling skills.

Segmentation and blending are essential skills for children to develop if they are to use their phonological knowledge to help them read unknown words and to help them in the spelling of new words. Working with onset and rime builds on the children's ability to hear and use rhyming words and to use this knowledge for reading and spelling. It will help them to develop the skill of making analogies between words or parts of words that are new to them. The following activity sheets will help children to become familiar with common rimes not only as they are used in short, relatively common words but as common elements in longer words that they will encounter as their reading and spelling progresses.

TASK 1 — ONSET AND RIME
A/S 71-81

Learning outcomes
- to segment words into onset and rime
- to blend onset and rime to produce a word
- to generate written word families

Instructions for Activity sheet 71
Look at the first picture and ask the pupil to name the picture (cat). Ask them to point to the initial phoneme and tell them the sound. Ask the pupil to look at the rime: 'at'. Look at the other two pictures and ask the pupil to name them: mat and rat. Ask the pupil if they rhyme and what the words have in common. Show the pupil the rime part of each word and ask them to say what phoneme needs to go at the beginning. Ask them to write each grapheme 'm' and 'r'. Look at the words again, pointing out the rime section and read the words aloud with the pupil.

Instructions for Activity sheet 72
Ask the pupil to read the rime element for each section or read it to them if they are unsure. Ask them to write the whole words on the lines provided and ask the pupil to read the words aloud. They could use one colour for the onset and another colour for the rime to help them see the pattern. Where appropriate ask the pupil to draw a picture to go with the words they have written.

Instructions for Activity sheets 73-75
Ask the pupil to read each word. Ask them to read the onset and rime of each word. Ask them to write as many words as they can in each word family on the lines provided. They should read each list aloud once they have completed the task.

Instructions for Activity sheets 76-77
These two sheet should be cut out. For longer wear they could be mounted on card and laminated. The cards can be used by an individual child to make as many real words as possible. The cards can be divided equally between two children to play a game as follows. Each child take it in turns to lay down a card. The other child must lay down a card that will make a real word. Once they have laid it down they should read the word. Scoring can be one point for laying down a correct card and one point for reading the word.

Instructions for Activity sheet 78
Cut out the two wheels and if necessary mount them on card and laminate. Place the smaller wheel on top of the larger one and secure in the centre. The pupil uses the word wheel to make and read as many words as possible. They can be recorded in the pupil's notebook.

Instructions for Activity sheets 79-80
The words should be cut out along the dotted lines. They can be mounted on card and laminated. Two, three or four children can play a game as follows. Each child takes it in turn to lay down a card, starting with a card that has the onset. Each child takes it in turn to lay down a piece of jigsaw so that it will make a real word. The child to put down all their cards is the winner. They should read each word as they lay down their card.

Instructions for Activity sheet 81
Fold the sheet as indicated by the fold numbers. Each fold reveals different onsets for the rime element of the words. The pupil reads the words and writes that word on the lines provided. The child should read all their words once they have finished.

Supporting activities
These activities use plastic letters and provide appropriate work prior to undertaking the activity sheets. You will need a large selection of plastic letters. It is particularly important to have extra vowels.
- Ask the child to make a simple cvc word with the plastic letters that they are likely to know how to spell e.g. hot.
- Ask them to make other words from this word, using the same rime e.g. cot. Let them make this word in any way they please.
- Ask them to make other words with the same rime e.g. pot, dot, got, lot, not, rot.
- Talk to the pupils about what they notice about the words, whether or not they rhyme. Read the list aloud. They should be able to see that the rime element is common to each word and that all the words rhyme. Continue with another rhyme family and hopefully they will see that they do not need to change the whole word every time but just the initial phoneme. The children can record their words or illustrate any appropriate ones.
- Start collecting word families to display on the classroom wall. Some are suitable for making an illustrated display e.g. man, fan, pan, can.
- Make class books of word families suitably illustrated. These can be used as a reference for the children when they are doing their own writing.

- Word families
Here are some word families to use in the activities:
Mat, cat, hat, bat, rat.
Fan man, pan, van.
Cap, map, tap.
Ten, men, hen, pen.
Bell, well, shell.
Bin, tin, pin, chin.
Lip, zip, ship, pip.
Hop, mop, stop, shop.
Lock, rock, sock.
Cot, pot, dot.
Bug, mug, rug, hug.
Bun, run, sun.
Wet, jet, net.
Ring, king, wing, swing.
Wig, pig.
Bed, red.
Leg, peg.
Box, fox.
Cake, lake, rake.
Coat, boat, goat.
Pill, till, hill.
Parrot, carrot.
Brick, stick, tick.

Name: _____ Date: _____

 cat

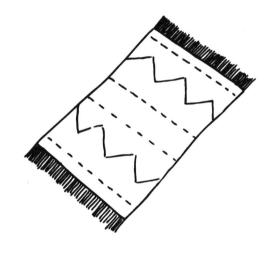 _at

 _at

cat _____ _____ _____

Activity sheet 71

Name: _____ Date: _____

w
l
m   ake
c
t

st
s
t   ick
l
br

r
f
l   ight
m
n

Activity sheet 72

Name: _____   Date: _____

chair
air

ring
ing

_____
_____
_____

_____
_____
_____

rake
ake

tent
ent

_____
_____
_____

_____
_____
_____

Activity sheet 73

Name: _____ Date: _____

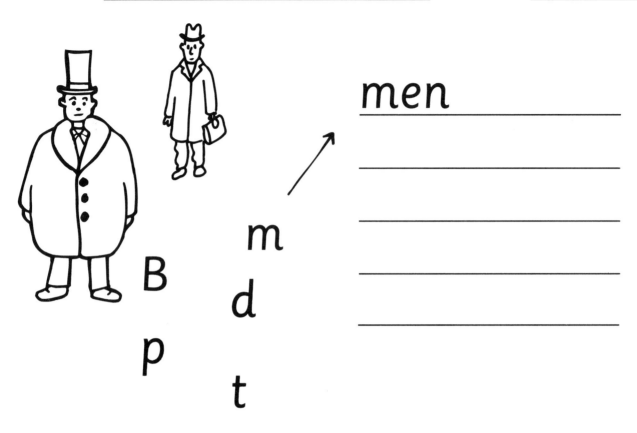

men _____
_____
_____
_____
_____

net _____
_____
_____
_____
_____
_____
_____

Activity sheet 74

Name: _____ Date: _____

cat

log

_____
_____
_____
_____

_____
_____
_____
_____

hen

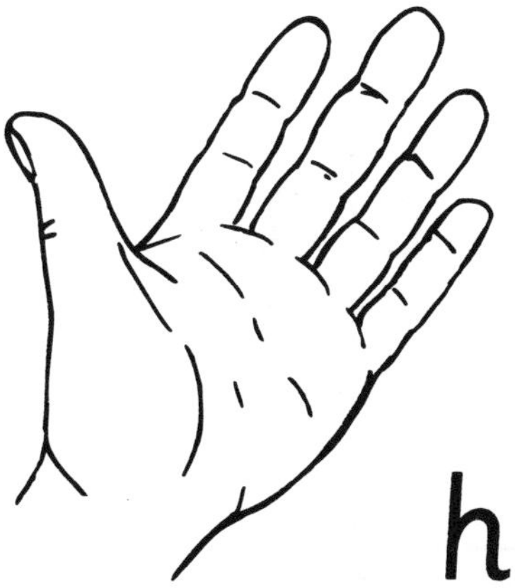

hand

_____
_____
_____
_____

_____
_____
_____
_____

Activity sheet 75

Name: _____ Date: _____

ot	f|ot	c|ot	p|ot
et	h|et	w|et	b|et
an	c|an	d|an	l|an
op	m|op	r|op	s|op

Activity sheet 76

en	ben	fen	pen
at	pat	pat	hat
ig	hig	mig	mig
ut	but	cut	cut

Activity sheet 77

Name: _____ Date: _____

Cut out to make a word wheel.

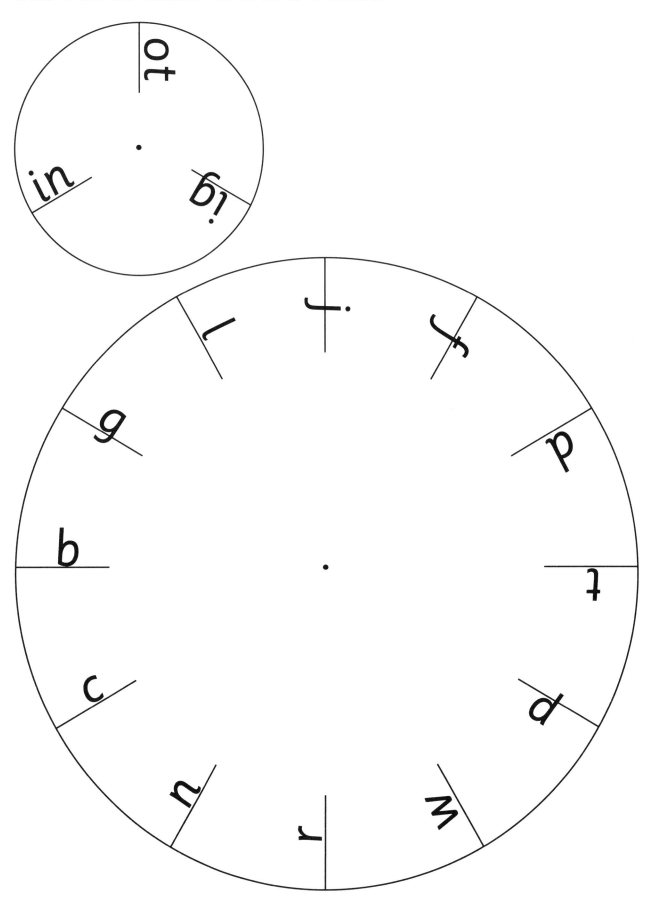

Activity sheet 78

Name: _____ Date: _____

c at

f at

b at

h at

t in

d in

w in

p in

Activity sheet 79

Name: _____ Date: _____

h) en | p) en

m) en | t) en

c) ot | h) ot

l) ot | p) ot

Activity sheet 80

Name: _____ Date: _____

c	b	f	m	en	an	in	at
r	p	m	h	en	an	in	at
f	t	p	t	en	an	in	at
cat							
rat							
fat							

fold 2   fold 3   fold 4   fold 1

Activity sheet 81

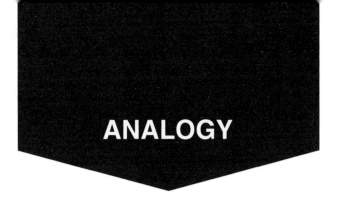

ANALOGY

Introduction
Usha Goswami (1995) has shown through her research that young children can and do make analogies between words or parts of words they know and words they do not know. Once children have established good rhyming skills and have had some experience with rhyming words written down, they are able to see that words that sound similar also look similar or have certain elements in common. This is a crucial skill and moves children on in both reading and spelling to new, unknown words. It is important to make pupils aware of the common rime elements as they appear not only in short familiar words but as parts of much longer words. It reinforces common letter strings and letters that are likely to 'go together' in the English language. It will also reduce the memory load when a pupil attempts to decode words. For example the word 'pancake' has six individual phonemes 'p', 'a', 'n', 'c', 'a–e', 'k'. If this is segmented into known elements it can become more manageable: 'p','an' 'c' ake' reduces it to four elements. The following activity sheets make the analogy quite explicit and also offer an opportunity to talk to the children about the similarities between words and how they can use this knowledge for themselves.

TASK 1 A/S 82-84

ANALOGY IN SPELLING

Learning outcomes
- to use analogy to spell new words

Instructions
The children complete the missing word using the word that is given in the sentence to make the analogy. The rime element that they need to use is underlined.

Supporting activities
- When hearing children read make a particular point of encouraging them to use analogy for decoding purposes.
- Using word family lists, change elements of the words to make them into new words. This may be the onset but it could also be the medial vowel or the final consonant. e.g. pot, pit, pet,. cat, cap, can.
- Ask the children to keep personal dictionaries of word families.
- Ask the children to generate lists of rhyming words to use for writing their own poetry or for writing a class poem around a theme.

Name: _____ Date: _____

10

The h<u>en</u> counted to _____

The m<u>an</u> had a _____

I can m<u>ake</u> a _____

The c<u>at</u> wore a _____

Activity sheet 82

Name: _____ Date: _____

The cl<u>ow</u>n wore a _____

 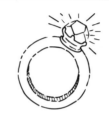

The k<u>ing</u> had a _____

 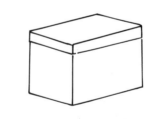

The f<u>ox</u> sat on a _____

The b<u>ee</u> flew into the _____

Activity sheet 83

Name: _____ Date: _____

The <u>m</u>ouse ran into his _____

The <u>fi</u>sh was on the _____

The <u>p</u>a<u>rr</u>ot ate a _____

 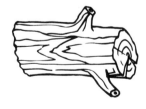

The <u>fr</u>o<u>g</u> sat on a _____

Activity sheet 84

INDIVIDUAL PHONEMES

Introduction
Children find working with individual phonemes relatively difficult. There are 44 phonemes in spoken language but these are represented by many more spelling choices. Children do need to develop the skill of hearing the individual phonemes in a word, as decoding when both reading and spelling are dependent on this. It may seem that good readers do not process words letter by letter but in practice disregarding individual letters would lead to many miscues. For example compete/complete, run/ruin, chase/case, etc. All these words require attention to individual phonemes and their graphemic representation. Skilled readers identify words on the basis of letter patterns which they link with sound patterns. Spoken words are produced which reveal the meaning. Once produced they can be checked against the context and interpreted.

TASK 1 — **COUNTING INDIVIDUAL PHONEMES** — A/S 85-90

Learning outcomes
- to hear and count the individual phonemes in a spoken word

Instructions for Activity sheets 85-86
Ask the pupil to name all the pictures to ensure they have identified them correctly. Ask the pupil to write how many phonemes they can hear in each word:
Sheet 84: c/a/t = 3, f/i/sh = 3, t/r/ee= 3, sh/ee/p = 3
Sheet 84: b/r/i/ck/s = 5, p/e/n/c/i/l = 6, t/a/b/le = 4, w/i/n/d/ow = 5, b/a/ll/oo/n = 5, f/l/ow/er = 4.

Instructions for Activity sheet 87
Name all the pictures before asking the pupil to undertake the activity sheet. Ask the pupils to sort the pictures into the correct box according to the number of phonemes in the word:
k/ey, s/aw, b/ee = 2 phonemes; d/o/g, t/i/ck, t/r/ee = 3 phonemes; p/r/a/m, f/r/o/g, f/l/ow/er = 4 phonemes.

Supporting activities
- Provide the pupils with a quantity of counters. Slowly read a list of words and ask the pupils to place a counter for each phoneme they can hear in each word. The words can be taken from their current reading material of from vocabulary being used in a class topic.
- Ask the pupils to make a graph of the numbers of phonemes there are in a set of words.
- Ask the pupils to count the number of phonemes in their own names and the names of their friends.

Instructions for Activity sheet 88-90
Ask the children to look at all the pictures on each page and ensure they are able to name them. Ask the children to circle the correct word.

Name: _____   Date: _____

How many phonemes in each word?

_____   _____

_____   _____

Activity sheet 85

Name: _____ Date: _____

How many phonemes in each word?

_____   _____

_____   _____

_____   _____

Activity sheet 86

Name: _____ Date: _____

Activity sheet 87

Name: _____ Date: _____

Circle the correct word.

fan pan	ham jam
red bed	rat sat
log dog	Sid lid

Activity sheet 88

Name: _____ Date: _____

Circle the correct word.

 ham hat	dot dog
 pin pit	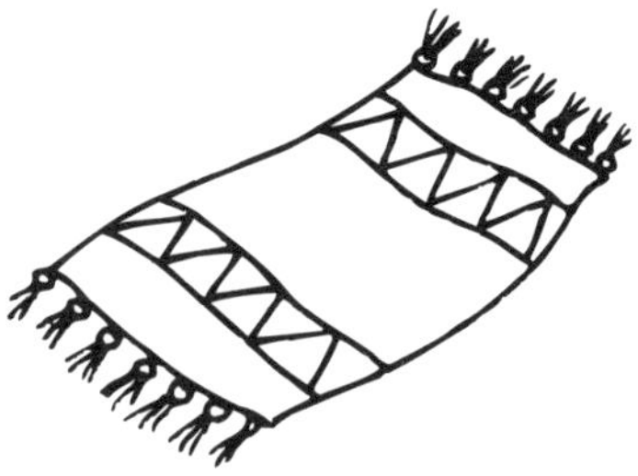 run rug
 pit pig	 map man

Activity sheet 89

Name: _____ Date: _____

Circle the correct word.

Activity sheet 90

ASSESSMENT

Name: _____

Can discriminate between environmental sounds.				
Understands and uses appropriate vocabulary e.g. soft, loud, high, low etc.				
Can discriminate between long and short words aurally.				
Understands and uses vocabulary: word, sentence, lower case, upper case etc.				
Can distinguish between upper and lower case letters.				
Can name lower case letters.				
Can name upper case letters.				
Can say the alphabet.				
Can sort words into alphabetical order.				
Can say how many syllables in a word.				
Can recite several common nursery rhymes.				
Can match rhyming words.				
Can generate rhyming words when provided with a cue word.				
Can match words starting with the same phoneme.				
Can generate words starting with the same phoneme.				
Can segment words into onset and rime.				
Can blend words when given the onset and rime orally.				
Can use analogy to generate new words for spelling.				
Can use analogy for decoding when reading.				
Can discriminate and count the individual phonemes in a word.				

The first three small boxes can be used when a pupil has undertaken a particular task. The final box can be used to demonstrate mastery of the skill.